No. 2739
$19.95

WORKING WITH
FIBERGLASS
TECHNIQUES AND PROJECTS

JACK WILEY

TAB BOOKS Inc.
Blue Ridge Summit, PA

FIRST EDITION
THIRD PRINTING

Printed in the United States of America

Library of Congress Cataloging in Publication Data

Wiley, Jack.
Working with fiberglass.

Includes index.
1. Fiberglass craft. I. Title.
TT297.8.w55   1986   745.5   86-5951
ISBN 0-8306-0739-0
ISBN 0-8306-2739-1 (pbk.)

TAB BOOKS Inc. offers software for
sale. For information and a catalog,
please contact TAB Software Department,
Blue Ridge Summit, PA 17294-0850.

Questions regarding the content of this book
should be addressed to:

Reader Inquiry Branch
TAB BOOKS Inc.
Blue Ridge Summit, PA 17294-0214

Contents

Introduction

This book is all about laminating and molding fiberglass reinforcing materials and plastic resins into interesting and useful projects. The term *laminating* refers to combining layers of reinforcing material and plastic resins into a solid material. *Molding* refers to shaping the fiberglass reinforcing materials and liquid resins into a solid material of the desired shape. While resin alone can be molded without fiberglass or other reinforcing material, this usually results in a brittle material and the process is usually called "casting" rather than "laminating."

Compared to traditional constructing materials like wood and metal, fiberglass is relatively new. It wasn't until the end of World War II that the chemistry and materials for fiberglass had developed to the point where practical applications were possible. The United States Navy and United States Coast Guard used fiberglass construction for making personnel boats. The use of fiberglass soon spread to the private sector, not only as a boatbuilding material, but also for furniture, tubs, tanks, lampshades, and even car bodies.

Over the years, fiberglass has been tried as a substitute for wood, metal, concrete, and other materials. As a construction material, fiberglass has both advantages and disadvantages. For some uses it proved feasible; for others it didn't. For some uses, it was too costly, or other materials had superior structural qualities or were easier to fabricate. For example, fiberglass is generally unsuitable for engine and mechanical constructions.

Fiberglass is often combined with other materials in order to take advantage of desirable characteristics of fiberglass, while avoiding its undesirable aspects for the particular application. For example, fiberglass car bodies generally make use of metal fasteners, hinges, latches, and trim and reinforcing members. Fiberglass tabletops and chairs often use metal legs. Metal fasteners are sometimes used for joining fiberglass moldings together. Thus, finished fiberglass laminates or moldings are a matrix of glass fibers and resin, which are in turn often combined with other materials to make functional and/or decorative objects.

Although many people do wood and metal working, there has been a reluctance to attempt fiberglass laminating and molding. One reason is the chemical aspect of fiberglassing. This is quite different from taking a piece of wood and cutting and shaping it. Fiberglass laminating and molding involves mixing chemicals together that are in liquid form, applying them to fiberglass reinforcing material over a form or in a mold, and by means of chemical reactions that take place within the liquid, coming up with a hard fiberglass laminate. While the exact chemistry is a mystery even to most experienced fiberglassers, the fact that a hard fiberglass laminate results is almost unimaginable to those who have not seen or done any fiberglassing.

A second reason why more people don't attempt their own fiberglass laminating and molding is the lack of how-to information. What tools, materials, and supplies are needed? How does one go about learning the techniques? What projects are suitable? This book is an attempt to provide the necessary information.

Health and aesthetic considerations are also responsible for the reluctance of many people to attempt fiberglass laminating and molding work. Precautions must, of course, be taken to guard health and safety when fiberglassing. The chemicals can be sticky and messy, and fiberglass reinforcing materials make your skin itch. By proper handling and use of protective clothing and equipment, it's possible to get around these problems, too.

Once you learn the basic techniques and safety procedures, fiberglassing can be enjoyable, challenging, and creative. The techniques presented in this book are intended primarily for the do-it-yourselfer, although they can be adapted for doing fiberglass laminating and molding as a business. There are two important differences. The do-it-yourselfer usually doesn't have to consider time as money, whereas the professional does. In most cases the professional has to work rapidly and efficiently to maximize the profits from his or her labor. With some experience and practice, the do-it-yourselfer can often achieve the same professional results. It will take longer to do the job, however.

The second important difference is that the professional generally has more and better tools and equipment than the typical do-it-yourselfer. The emphasis in this book is on doing quality work with a limited amount of tools and equipment, since the do-it-yourselfer usually has to absorb the cost of the tools and equipment with a limited number of projects, whereas the professional can spread this cost over hundreds of moldings.

In *The Fiberglass Repair and Construction Handbook* (TAB book No. 1297), I cover making repairs to existing fiberglass products, using fiberglassing techniques to repair other materials, and constructing things from preformed fiberglass panels and kits. This book focuses on making things out of fiberglass from scratch, including furniture, toys, ponds, lamps, and a variety of other functional and/or decorative items. Various laminating and molding techniques are covered. The emphasis is on projects using molds that you can make from inexpensive materials.

Chapter 1

Overview

Fiberglass reinforced plastic (FRP) is now commonly called *fiberglass*. Originally, the term referred to the thin glass fibers or filaments. While fiberglass is still used to refer to these glass fibers, as well as reinforcing materials such as mat and woven fabrics made from these fibers, it also refers to a two-part structural unit consisting of glass fibers combined with a plastic resin—usually polyester and sometimes epoxy.

Fiberglass reinforced plastic (FRP) refers, in the plastic industry, to a two-part structural unit; "fiberglass reinforced" is the glass fiber reinforcement and "plastic" is the resin. This terminology is seldom used outside the plastics industry. Most people refer to a hot tub, chair, car body, swimming pool, and other objects made out of fiberglass reinforced plastic as being fiberglass.

REASONS FOR DOING YOUR
OWN FIBERGLASS LAMINATING AND MOLDING

Before going into the actual techniques for fiberglass laminating and molding construction projects, it is important to take a look at some of the reasons for doing this work yourself.

Perhaps the most important reason is to save money. The price of manufactured fiberglass products varies depending on the demand for the particular item, the number produced, and other factors. On items such as fiberglass bathtubs and shower stalls, it is very difficult to build

1

your own for less than the price of the manufactured items, because they are produced in large numbers and sold to a highly competitive market. However, many other manufactured products are made in limited numbers and sold at relatively higher prices, and it is here that money can be saved by making your own.

You can save money not only by providing your own labor, but also by being able to purchase materials and supplies from discount supply firms.

By doing your own fiberglass laminating and molding, you can make items that fit your exact needs, including projects that are not available in manufactured versions. Once you learn the basic techniques, fiberglass can be molded into almost any desired shape or form. There are tremendous possibilities for making custom or original constructions.

Some people only do their own fiberglass laminating and molding work to save money, others relish the challenge and derive satisfaction from doing this work themselves. Fiberglass laminating and molding is a proven method for making challenging and creative items.

ADVANTAGES AND DISADVANTAGES OF FIBERGLASS

For some uses, fiberglass has proven itself to be a superior or at least competitive material compared to other possible building materials. For other uses, fiberglass could not compete—for various reasons.

Advantages

Cured fiberglass (fiberglass reinforced plastic) does not corrode or rot. It is inert to most common chemicals, including most fuels and common pollutants. This makes it ideal for items subject to severe environmental conditions. A steel tabletop used outdoors, for example, will rust; one of fiberglass won't. Fiberglass is chemically inert to most common chemicals, an important advantage for use in or around salt water or marine environments.

Fiberglass is strong and lightweight. When properly designed and fabricated from quality materials, it has approximately the same structural strength as wood or steel weighing twice as much.

Fiberglass can be molded in one-piece seamless forms that are leak-proof, making it ideal for tubs, pools, tanks, boat hulls, and other similar items. Fiberglass can be molded into complex shapes. This is fairly easy to do and allows shapes and designs that are difficult to achieve from wood or metal. There are limits to the shapes that can be molded using standard molding techniques. Some fiberglass constructions do have seams and lap joints, although these can often be fiberglass bonded. In some cases mechanical fasteners, with or without fiberglass bonding, are used.

By means of a resin gel coat or other means, colors can be molded into the fiberglass. This allows for many creative possibilities.

Fiberglass is durable. When properly fabricated, fiberglass laminates will last for 30 years and perhaps much longer with no significant decline in laminate properties. Fiberglass requires relatively little maintenance because of its noncorrosive nature.

Fiberglass can be engineered to make maximum use of the material. Various laminate thicknesses can be used on the same molding to give strength and stiffness where it is needed. A thinner laminate can be used to save weight in areas where less strength and stiffness will be adequate.

There is little waste of materials in most fiberglass molding methods. Most of the resin and reinforcing material ends up as part of the finished product. In wood and steel construction, for example, there are almost always scrap pieces. Fiberglass molding is largely a chemical construction method, rather than building from preformed materials. It is relatively easy to vary thicknesses to give strength as required, something that is often difficult to do with wood or metal.

Disadvantages

Fiberglass laminates have less stiffness than steel and even aluminum. This can cause problems in applications where deflections can cause failure. The fatigue strength of fiberglass is lower than that of steel, which can cause problems in areas where stress concentrations are located. The buckling strength of fiberglass is also low. Various stiffening members, however, can often be added to the fiberglass laminate to get around these problems.

Fiberglass has less abrasion resistance than steel, but better abrasion resistance than most woods. In fiberglass areas where chafing may occur, various types of protective devices made from metal, rubber, or other materials can be used.

Unless special, more expensive, fire-retardant resins are used, fiberglass is vulnerable to fire. It is similar to wood in that respect.

The high cost of fiberglass construction is a disadvantage. The cost of steel and wood construction is generally less on a pound-per-pound basis than fiberglass. For many applications, however, various desirable features of fiberglass make it worth the additional cost.

The tooling and construction of molds for manufactured products is often costly. This cost can be amortized if the same mold is used for large numbers of moldings. The do-it-yourselfer often wants to make just one or a limited number. An important part of this book is methods for making inexpensive molds for a variety of interesting construction projects.

FIBERGLASS REINFORCED PLASTIC

Some plastics, such as nylon, can be changed from solid to liquid state by heat. These are called *thermoplastic*, and become solid again as they cool.

Other plastics, including polyester and epoxy resins (the two types most commonly used to form fiberglass reinforced plastic), are liquid only in their formative state. They cure into a solid state and are then not affected by heat unless it is high enough for them to burn. These resins are termed *thermosetting*. They are set or cured by heat, which can either be applied chemically from inside the resin (exothermic heat), or outside, or a combination.

Polyester and epoxy resins, the two types of main concern in this book, are rather brittle when used alone, but form a strong and rigid composite material when a suitable reinforcing material, such as glass fibers, is added. These materials can be set or cured in a mold to desired shape. Once in a solid state, they cannot be reformed to a new shape by heat, but they can be sawed and machined.

PROJECTS YOU CAN MAKE

The fact that fiberglass reinforced plastic can be formed to the shape of a mold means that you can make many domestic and hobby items from this material, including model boats, flower pots, garden furniture, and garden pools and fountains. This book details not only a variety of laminating and molding techniques, but also gives complete plans and directions for making a variety of functional and/or decorative objects. No prior knowledge of fiberglassing is assumed. If you have had no previous fiberglassing experience, you can begin with small easy projects, such as those involving flat or shallow curved molds, and then work up to larger and more difficult projects, such as a garden pool.

Chapter 2

Materials and Supplies

Materials and supplies for both fiberglass laminating and making the molds are discussed here.

REINFORCING MATERIALS

The reinforcing material is one part of a two-part structural unit that forms fiberglass (fiberglass reinforced plastic). Glass fibers are most commonly used as the reinforcing material. Many new reinforcing materials have been developed in recent years. For certain uses, these have qualities superior to glass fibers. Even though a laminate may have no glass fibers in it, it is still commonly referred to as fiberglass. I will follow this practice, although all of the projects detailed here can be made using glass reinforcing material.

Glass Fiber Reinforcing Materials

Glass fiber is a fairly new synthetic, dating back to the early 1930s. Lime, alumina (aluminum oxide), and borosilicate are used to form E glass. The E glass is melted and formed into continuous filaments by mechanical attenuation. Molten glass is pulled through small holes in the bottom of an electrical furnace and stretched into thin fibers, which are made into yarns. These yarns are then formed into glass fiber reinforcing materials by weaving on regular weaving machinery or other means.

To make the glass fiber reinforcing material suitable for use with plas-

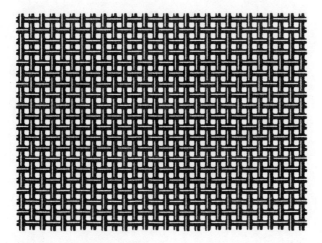

Fig. 2-1. Fiberglass cloth with plain weave.

tic resins, special finishes (usually chroming) are added to the glass fibers. These allow the plastic resins to flow around the glass fibers and minimize trapped air during laminating and molding. Glass fiber reinforcing material is available commercially in many forms including cloth, mat, woven roving, chopped strands, combination chopped strands and woven roving, and milled fibers.

Glass Fiber Cloth

Glass fiber cloth is made by weaving threads made of glass fibers into cloth using regular textile weaving machinery. Many different weaves are used, with a plain weave (Fig. 2-1), long shaft satin weave (Fig. 2-2), and unidirectional weave (Fig. 2-3) being most commonly used for fiberglass laminating and molding. The plain weave, which is the most common type and usually the least expensive, can be used for most of the projects detailed in this book that require cloth reinforcing material. There are a few projects, however, where the long shaft satin, which gives a smooth surface, and unidirectional weave, which gives greater reinforcing strength in one direction, are required.

Glass fiber cloth is available not only in various weaves, but also in various weights per square yard. Weights from about 2 ounces per square yard up to about 20 ounces per square yard are useful for various types of laminating and molding work. Weights from about 6 to 10 ounces are used for most of the projects except for models and small items, which require lighter weights. (These are dry weights of the cloth before it has been saturated with plastic resin.)

Fig. 2-2. Fiberglass cloth with long shaft satin weave.

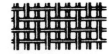

Fig. 2-3. Fiberglass cloth with unidirectional weave.

When used to make fiberglass laminates, cloth gives the most strength but the least thickness. It usually takes 40 to 50 layers of 10 ounces per square yard cloth to make a 1-inch thick laminate.

Cloth is available by the yard in widths from about 38 to 60 inches with *selvaged* edges (Fig. 2-4) so that it will not unravel. Cloth tape with selvaged edges is available in widths from 1 to 12 inches.

The selvaged edges make the cloth easier to handle, so the width should be selected for the particular molding job. At the unselvaged ends and where cuts are made, the cloth will tend to unravel. It must be handled carefully when dry and when plastic resin is being applied to it.

Cloth is a fairly easy reinforcing material to lay up in a mold on a flat surface, but it is difficult to keep wrinkle-free in curved areas. Cuts are usually made to form square corners and various other configurations. Cloth gives a fairly smooth finish, especially if lighter weight clots are used.

Figure 2-5 shows a cloth laminate. Cloth requires the least resin of all the reinforcing fabric, which makes a strong laminate. However, it lacks stiffness. Also, it does not give good waterproofing because of the limited amount of resin. It's resin rather than reinforcing material that makes fiberglass reinforced plastic highly impervious to water. To get around this problem when waterproofing is required, cloth is usually combined with mat reinforcing material (described later in this chapter), which takes more resin.

Cloth is usually the most expensive of the reinforcing materials on a weight basis. For some users in laminating and molding, it has advantages that make it worth the additional cost.

Since untreated glass fiber cloth is also available, it's extremely important that you purchase only the kind specially treated for resin. Be

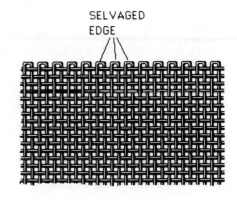

SELVAGED
EDGE

Fig. 2-4. Cloth with selvaged edge.

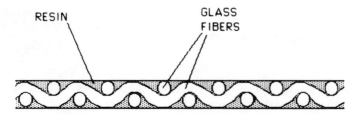

RESIN

GLASS
FIBERS

Fig. 2-5. Fiberglass cloth laminate.

careful about "bargains" in fiberglass cloth. The material may be un-chromed and thus unsuitable for fiberglass laminating and molding. The chroming gives the cloth a shiny appearance; untreated fabric has a dull appearance.

Unlike most woven materials, glass fiber cloth has a slip weave that allows the threads to slide over each other. This allows individual strands to slip over each other so that the dry fabric can be shaped to compound curves in one piece without cutting it. However, there are definite limits to the amount of compound curving that can be accomplished in a mold in this manner.

Fiberglass cloth can be purchased by the roll, by the yard cut to the desired length from a roll, and precut to small sizes in packages. A straight cut can be made by cutting and pulling out one strand that goes across the cloth. This will serve as a guideline for cutting the fabric with scissors or shears.

Glass Fiber Mat

Glass fiber mat is manufactured by laying down chopped strands of glass fiber in a random pattern on a flat surface. A bonding agent is used to bond the strands together into a feltlike material (Fig. 2-6).

Unlike cloth and woven roving (described below), mat is sold in weights per square foot rather than per square yard. Mat is commonly available in weights ranging from about 1/2 ounce per square foot to 3 ounces per square foot. It is available in widths from about 36 to 60 inches. It can be purchased by the roll, by the yard cut from a roll or in small sizes precut in packages.

Mat is the least expensive of the reinforcing materials on a weight basis. This advantage is partially offset by the fact that it requires more

Fig. 2-6. Fiberglass mat is feltlike material.

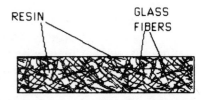

RESIN   GLASS
FIBERS

Fig. 2-7. Mat laminate.

resin than cloth or woven roving. Like cloth, woven roving, and other glass fiber reinforcing materials, mat must be treated, such as by chroming, before it is suitable for use with plastic resins.

Mat has a lower glass per resin ratio, usually from 25 to 35 percent, than cloth or woven roving laminates. Because of the high proportion of resin in the mat laminate, it yields a weaker laminate than either cloth or woven roving. Mat has the advantage of forming the stiffest laminate. Also, because of its nondirectional random pattern, it has the best inner bonding strength when used in a laminate (Fig. 2-7).

Because of its high resin content, a mat laminate has the best water-proofness. It forms a much better barrier against water than either cloth or woven roving.

Mat is frequently used for filling in the coarse weave pattern of woven roving when laying up a molding, reducing the amount of resin without reinforcing glass fibers and increasing the strength of the resulting laminate (Fig. 2-8).

For many fiberglass laminating and molding uses, mat is the easiest material to use. It is easy to wet out or saturate with resin. While dry mat is generally fairly stiff and will not shape to compound curves in a mold, when wetted out or saturated with plastic resin, the binder holding the mat together dissolves. This allows the mat to be shaped easily to compound curves and other configurations.

Care must be taken when applying wet resin to mat to prevent it from bunching up and forming lumps. However, this is seldom much of a problem after the correct techniques for laying up mat (as detailed in later chapters) have been learned.

It might appear that the short strands of chopped fibers, usually from

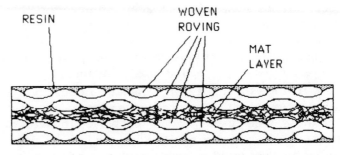

RESIN   WOVEN
ROVING

MAT
LAYER

Fig. 2-8. Mat used in laminate between layers of woven roving to fill in coarse weave pattern.

about 3/4 to 1 1/2 inches in length, are responsible for making mat laminates weaker than cloth and woven roving laminates that have long continuous strands of glass fibers. However, tests indicate that this has only a slight effect on the strength of the laminate, and that the mat laminate is weaker mainly because of the lower glass to resin ratio.

For many of the projects in this book, either mat or cloth can be used to achieve about the same results. In this case, I recommend that mat be used, because it is much easier to wet out or saturate with resin and air bubbles are seldom much of a problem, as they are when using cloth. This point will become clear when you do fiberglass laminating and molding work.

In a laminate, it takes about 20 layers of 1 1/2-ounce-per square-foot (dry weight) mat to build up a 1-inch thickness. Because of the higher resin content and resulting lower strength and modulus of elasticity, mat laminates must be thicker than those of cloth or woven roving to have equivalent properties.

Surfacing Mat

Surfacing mat is a special-purpose mat formed from individual glass fibers rather than whole strands. It has a thin body and gives a very smooth surface. It is useful for surfacing and overlay work. For example, when regular mat is used to build up a laminate, a layer of surfacing mat can be added to give a smooth surface. It is also used to make lampshades and other items requiring a thin, smooth material. The glass fibers can be seen through the resin, giving an interesting effect.

Surfacing mat is available in thicknesses from about .01 to .03 inch and in widths from about 38 to 60 inches. It is sold by the roll, which usually has about 200 yards, or by the linear yard cut from a roll. Surfacing mat is also sold in plastic packages, which usually contain about a square yard of the material. Surfacing mat is used for some of the projects detailed in this book.

Glass Fiber Woven Roving

Glass fiber woven roving has a coarse weave pattern (Fig. 2-9). Whereas cloth is made from glass fiber thread that is twisted like yarn, roving is continuous strands of glass fibers that are grouped together. Woven roving is a thick, clothlike reinforcing material. Woven roving is generally only used in large laminates where great strength is required. While woven roving is available in various weights per square yard, 24 ounces per square yard (dry weight) is that most common.

Figure 2-10 shows a single-layer laminate. About 25 layers of 24 ounces of woven roving with 24 ounces to the square yard will give about an inch thickness. When used in laminates, woven roving is almost always alternated with layers of mat to fill in the heavy weave pattern. This combination gives good adhesion, stiffness, and tensile strength.

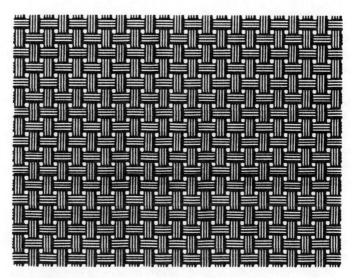

Fig. 2-9. Woven roving.

Woven roving is available by the yard in widths from about 38 to 60 inches. The woven roving comes with unselvaged edges, which requires careful handling so that it will not unravel.

Woven roving can be purchased by the roll or by the yard cut to desired length from the roll. Care should be taken when cutting woven roving to prevent unraveling. Woven roving is also sometimes sold in plastic bags, usually with about a square yard of the material.

On a weight basis, woven roving is more expensive than mat, but less expensive than cloth. The woven roving has the advantage over cloth in that it gives a more rapid buildup of thickness. Because of the heavy basket weave, woven roving does not give as smooth a surface as cloth.

A main disadvantage of woven roving as compared to both cloth and mat is that the woven roving is more difficult to wet out and saturate with resin. Woven roving requires more resin than cloth. A woven roving laminate is generally about 45 percent glass fibers and 55 percent resin, whereas a cloth laminate is generally about 50 percent glass fibers and 50 percent plastic resin. Both woven roving and cloth require much less resin than mat.

Because of the relatively low resin content, woven roving, like cloth,

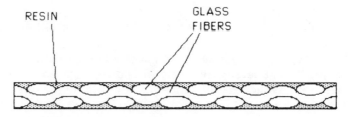

Fig. 2-10. Single-layer woven roving laminate.

gives a laminate that lacks waterproofness. To get around this problem, woven roving is usually combined with mat, which takes more resin, in laminates requiring waterproofness. It's the resin and not the reinforcing material that makes fiberglass highly impervious to water.

Like cloth reinforcing material, woven roving has a slip weave. This allows the rovings to slide over each other to a certain extent. Individual strands slip over each other, so the dry fabric can be shaped to compound curves in one piece in a mold without cutting it. However, there are definite limits to the amount of compound curving that can be accomplished. The heavy weight and thick basket weave makes woven roving generally much more difficult to work with than cloth.

Chopped Glass Fiber Strands

Chopped strands of glass fiber rovings are another important glass fiber reinforcement for fiberglassing laminating and molding work. They are available in lengths from about 1/4 to 2 inches. The glass fiber must be chrome treated before it is suitable for fiberglassing work. Chopped strands are usually sold in packages by weight.

Chopped strands are added to resin to give structural strength. However, they generally produce a weaker laminate than glass fiber cloth, woven roving, or mat. The chopped strands should be thought of as a supplement to, rather than a replacement for, these other reinforcing materials.

When using chopped strands, keep the ratio of chopped strands high in relation to the amount of resin used. This will result in the greatest structural strength and will help keep the resulting material from being overly brittle because of too large a percentage of resin.

Combination Woven Roving and Chopped Strands or Mat

Woven roving and chopped strands or mat combined into a single material are also available. This combination material is a time-saver for fast buildup of large fiberglass moldings. However, this material is not required for the projects detailed in this book. The main advantage is that a layer of woven roving and chopped strands or mat is laid up in one operation, which cuts the labor cost in manufacturing operations. The main disadvantages are that the material is difficult to handle and wet out or saturate with resin. It's usually much easier to first lay up a layer of one of these reinforcing materials, followed by a layer of the other material, than to use the combination material, although it will probably take longer.

Various weights are available, with about 24 ounces per square yard being typical. It is generally available in widths from about 38 to 60 inches. Like cloth, woven roving, and mat, it's sold by the roll or by the linear yard from a roll.

Milled Fibers

Milled fibers, sometimes called ground fibers, are made from glass strands. These are hammer-milled into pieces much shorter than chopped strands.

These fibers are usually sold in packages by weight. Some large suppliers sell them by the pound in bulk.

Milled fibers can be added to polyester or epoxy resins to form a jellylike paste that makes an excellent filler material. The consistency of the compound can be controlled by the amount of milled fibers added to the resin. A lesser amount of these fibers can be added to resin as a thickening material to keep the resin from running down or sagging when doing fiberglassing layup work on vertical or overhead surfaces.

Milled fibers mixed with resin usually do not result in as much structural strength as when chopped strands are similarly used. Thus, the milled fibers mixed with resin should be used only for filling in small areas.

NONFIBERGLASS REINFORCING MATERIALS

Several nonfiberglass reinforcing materials, including Vectra Polypropylene, Dynel Modacrylic fiber, Xynole polyester, DuPont Kevlar 49 Aramid, and carbon fiber, are now available for use with polyester and epoxy resins. These nonfiberglass reinforcing materials are generally more expensive (some of them much more expensive) than glass fibers. For some types of constructions, however, they have advantages that make them worth the additional cost.

Laminates made up of these nonfiberglass reinforcing materials and plastic resin are often referred to as fiberglass, even though there are no glass fibers in the material. This broad use of the term "fiberglass" is used in this book.

Vectra Polypropylene

Vectra polypropylene reinforcing material is made from an extremely lightweight textile fiber. Standard polypropylene cloth at 4.3 ounces per square yard has about the same bulk and absorption as 10-ounce fiberglass cloth. Polypropylene has a higher strength-to-weight ratio than fiberglass reinforcing material. It possesses useful attributes: it is lightweight and has high tensile strength. Other advantages include greater abrasion resistance, greater elasticity, and better bonding adhesion to wood than fiberglass reinforcements. Unlike fiberglass reinforcing materials, polypropylene does not cause skin irritation during handling and sanding and is nonallergenic. This is an extremely important advantage for those who are allergic to glass fiber reinforcing materials.

Disadvantages of polypropylene include higher cost (approximately one or two dollars a yard more than 10 ounces per square yard fiber-glass cloth, which has about the same bulk and absorption of resin as 4.3-ounces-per-square-yard polypropylene), a tendency to hold its creases, and a tendency to float in wet resin, making it somewhat diffi-cult to lay down without the formation of air bubbles. The high abra-sion resistance of moldings laid up with polypropylene make it resistive to sanding.

Polypropylene is easy to work with in many ways. The greater elastic-ity allows easy application around compound curves. The material wets out rapidly and easily.

The greater elasticity of polypropylene makes it better suited than fiberglass reinforcing materials for surfaces that can be worked. How-ever, to prevent cracking of the resin, special flexible polyester or ep-oxy resin (readily available but slightly more expensive than regular resin) should be used.

Polypropylene cloth reinforcing material is available by the roll or by the linear yard from rolls in widths from 38 to 60 inches. Fabric count is 21 × 21 in a spun plied yarn construction. Large openings in weave allow for penetration of resin during layup. The cloth has selvaged edges.

Polypropylene is also available in tape form in widths from 2 to 12 inches. "Tape" is a narrow strip of the cloth fabric; there is no adhesive backing. The edges of the polypropylene tape presently available do not have selvaged edges. They are machine cut. Care must be taken in han-dling the tape so that it does not become unraveled.

Dynel Acrylic

Dynel is an acrylic reinforcing fabric. The acrylic yarn is made in Japan, and the finished yarn is woven into fabric in the United States. It's avail-able in a 4 ounces per square yard dry weight in a 63-inch width. It is sold by the roll or by the linear yard cut from rolls. It is presently usually priced slightly higher than the polypropylene fabric.

Dynel acrylic fabric weighs only about half as much as fiberglass cloth of the same thickness. The main advantages of the acrylic, as com-pared to fiberglass, are greater abrasion resistance, higher tensile strength, and the fact that it does not cause skin irritation when han-dled or sanded. The acrylic fabric is fairly easy to work with; it is easier to stretch around sharp corners and curves than either fiberglass or poly-propylene reinforcing fabric. It provides a slick finish when sanded, mak-ing it ideal for use as an overlay. A canvaslike finish is possible by using a minimum of resin. In either case, the fabric is easy to wet out. The main use of Dynel acrylic fabric is as an overlay for a fiberglass laminate to provide greater abrasion resistance. The acrylic fabric provides much bet-ter adhesion to wood than does fiberglass, although not quite as good as does the polypropylene fabric described previously. Both polyester and epoxy resins can be used with the Dynel acrylic fabric.

14

Xynole Polyester

Xynole polyester is an ultrafast wet out reinforcing and overlay fabric. It is generally considered to be the easiest reinforcing material to apply. It conforms easily to compound curves and wets out easily and rapidly without leaving air bubbles.

Other advantages of Xynole polyester as compared to fiberglass are that Xynole polyester does not cause skin irritation from handling or sanding and has better laminating adhesion with either polyester or epoxy resin. Also, Xynole polyester has greater toughness and abrasion resistance and better weight-to-strength ratio.

The main disadvantage of Xynole polyester is that it lacks stiffness. For this reason, it is usually not used alone for laminating in areas where high stresses will exist. It makes an ideal overlay for fiberglass reinforced laminates and as a waterproof coating for plywood and metal.

Xynole polyester is available in a 4.2-ounces-per-square-yard dry weight cloth, which has about the same bulk and absorption of resin as 10-ounces-per-square-yard dry weight fiberglass reinforcing cloth. It is available by the roll or by the linear yard cut from rolls in widths from 38 to 60 inches. Xynole polyester is usually priced only slightly higher than 10-ounces-per-square-yard fiberglass cloth. It is also available in tape form in widths from 1 1/2 to 12 inches.

DuPont Kevlar Reinforcing Material

Kevlar is a synthetic long-chain polymer fiber developed by DuPont in 1972. It is now available in a 5-ounces-per-square-yard reinforcing fabric in 38- and 50-inch widths. This material can be used with polyester or epoxy resin. Laminates from this material have greater tensile strength than when fiberglass reinforcement is used, but they are not as strong in compression or bending. An important advantage is superior impact strength. A big disadvantage of this material for fiberglass laminating and molding work is that it is much more expensive than fiberglass reinforcing material.

Carbon Fiber Reinforcing Material

Carbon fiber reinforcing material is available for use with epoxy resin for laminating purposes. It gives high strength with minimum weight, but is very expensive.

RESINS

While there are many types of resins that can be combined with reinforcing materials to form reinforced plastic (commonly called fiberglass), our concern here will be with only the two main ones: polyester and epoxy. All of the fiberglass laminating and molding projects detailed in this book can be accomplished with these resins. Other types, such as silicone, phenolic, melamine, and thermoplastic resins, while useful in some manufacturing processes, will not be required.

Polyester Resins

Polyester resin is a thermosetting plastic, which means that it is set or cured by heat. The heat can either be applied chemically from inside the resin (exothermic heat) or outside, or some combination of the two can be used. An accelerator (a highly active oxidizing material) and a catalyst are added to the liquid polyester resin to start the chemical reaction that causes the internal heat. The heat is the setting agent. When polyester resin is in liquid form, the molecules lay side by side in no set pattern. The addition of heat causes the molecules to link together in chains to form a solid plastic—a hard mass that cannot be softened by application of heat. The process of changing from a liquid to a solid is called *polymerization*.

Most of the polyester resins that are manufactured for room temperature cures, the ones that will be used for most fiberglass laminating and molding work, already have the necessary accelerator added to the liquid resin. In most cases the accelerator is cobalt naphthenate. Only a catalyst, usually methyl-ethyl-ketone (MEK) peroxide, need be added to the polyester resin to start the cure at room temperature.

Polyester resin will harden at room temperature in time even without the addition of the catalyst. With the catalyst, however, the resin hardens quickly—usually in about five minutes to an hour, depending on how much catalyst is added, room temperature, humidity and other factors. The thickness of the layer of resin applied also affects the rate of cure. A thick layer keeps the heat inside better, causing it to cure faster than a thin layer.

The fact that polyester resin will harden in time at room temperature means that liquid polyester resin, even when in sealed containers, has a limited shelf life. When purchasing resin, always make sure that it is fresh and has not started to cure in the container.

Laminating and Finishing Polyester Resins

Many types of polyester resins have been developed for specific purposes. The two types commonly used for fiberglass laminating and molding are: laminating or lay-up and finishing or surfacing.

The laminating or lay-up resin is air-inhibited, which means that in the presence of air it will not fully cure. The surface will remain tacky. This condition is desirable when additional layers of fiberglass are to be added to a laminate, because there is no waxy surface to prevent laminating additional resin layers together properly.

Finishing or surfacing resin is non-air-inhibited, which means that it will fully cure in the presence of air. This is desirable for final application to a laminate when a complete cure is wanted, such as for the final layer of a molding. Non-air-inhibited resin has a wax or similar ingredient added. When the catalyzed resin is added to a laminate, the wax rises to the surface, sealing off the air and allowing a complete cure. The surface can then be sanded (the tacky surface that results when air-inhibited resin is used will quickly gum up sandpaper).

Laminating or lay-up polyester resin can be made to cure tackfree by adding a special wax to the liquid resin before application. Still another method of achieving a surface cure when laminating or lay-up resin is used is to seal the surface from the air. One way to do this is to cover the surface with cellophane, taping it in place around the edges or otherwise securing it so that air cannot get below.

When finishing or surface resin is used, it cures with a waxy surface. If for any reason another layer of laminate must be added to this, the wax should first be removed. This can be accomplished by means of sanding or by using a solvent, such as acetone.

A general-purpose resin that can be used for both laminating or lay-up, and finishing or surfacing work is also available. Some fiberglass workers look down at this resin, saying that it doesn't do either job well. I have achieved satisfactory results with it for many types of fiberglassing work—that is, provided that I used quality brands. However, for large jobs I highly recommend the use of both laminating and finishing resins, or using a wax additive to make finishing resin from laminating resin—rather than using a general-purpose resin.

High-Viscosity Polyester Resins

Polyester resins are available with either regular or high viscosity. The high-viscosity resins contain a thixotropic or thickening agent that helps to eliminate dripping and sagging on vertical and overhead surfaces. Special thixotropic powder is available for adding to regular resin to give it a higher viscosity. Some types actually strengthen the resin. Avoid the use of clay and inert earth as a thixotropic agent, because these will weaken the cured resin. Thixotropic powder suitable for use with both polyester and epoxy resins is sold in bags or containers by weight or in bulk by weight.

Flexible Polyester Resins

Polyester resins have various degrees of flexibility when cured. Some are very rigid when cured; others are quite flexible. Most are somewhere in between. Special flexible polyester resin is recommended for use with the nonfiberglass reinforcing materials that stretch or elongate more than fiberglass reinforcing materials do. Flexible resins result in a laminate that will crack or craze (form tiny surface cracks) less. More rigid resins should be used when greater stiffness is desired.

Fire-Retardant Polyester Resin

Cured laminates made up of regular polyester resin will support combustion about the same as plywood. Special fire-retardant polyester resin is available. It's more expensive than the regular resin, but this extra cost is warranted for use in constructions requiring fire retardancy. The fire retardancy is achieved by co-reactant compound that is combined with the liquid resin. This results in a slower curing time for the resin—but adhesion, flexibility, and impact resistance are not affected. The co-reactant adds a white opacity to the resin, and the usual translucency is lost.

Polyester Resins and Temperature

Most polyester resins are formulated for use in a temperature range from about 70 to 75 degrees Fahrenheit. Satisfactory results can generally be achieved in a temperature range from 60 to 70 degrees Fahrenheit by adding additional catalyst, and by adding less catalyst in a temperature range from 75 to 90 degrees Fahrenheit. This will be explained in detail later. For now it's important to realize that regular polyester resin is suitable for use in a Fahrenheit temperature range of from about 60 to 90 degrees, with difficulties increasing near the extremes.

Special low-temperature resin is available that has been specially formulated for use in a temperature range from about 45 to 60 degrees Fahrenheit. This will allow satisfactory fiberglass laminating and molding work to be done at these colder temperatures. This is a pre-accelerated resin (an accelerator has already been added by the manufacturer to the liquid resin) that is catalyzed in the same manner as regular polyester resin. The shelf life of low-temperature resin is limited to three or four months, and the entire contents of the container should be used by that time.

Gel Coat Polyester Resin

Still another type of polyester resin is gel coat. Its main use is to form the protective color gel coat surface on a fiberglass molding. It's available in clear form for adding your own pigment or with the color already added. Most gel coat resin is air-inhibited. It is applied over a mold release agent in the mold on the side that will be the finished side. The lay-up of resin and reinforcing materials follows. The gel coat will form the outside color surface on the finished molding and cures because it is air-inhibited against the mold. It will also cure when sealed off from the air by wax or other covering. Gel coat resin is specially formulated to give a protective, waterproof color coat.

For touching up small areas of gel coat, it is usually easier to use non-air-inhibited resin so that it will cure in air. Color pigments available in liquid, paste, and powder forms can be used with polyester or epoxy resin. The paste form is generally easiest to mix and blend.

Special gel coat spray kits are available for gel coat touchup work. Kits are also available for mixing and matching colors. Methods for applying the gel coat include: knife, brush, and spray.

Polyester gel coat resin is catalyzed in the same manner as regular polyester resin. Since the gel coat forms a layer without reinforcement inside, it must be a thin layer if cracking and crazing are to be prevented.

Water Clear Polyester Casting Resin

Another type of resin that has uses in molding, especially for hobby and craft work, is water clear polyester casting resin. This resin is well suited for encapsulating biological and geological specimens, making decorative castings, and similar uses. Either opaque or transparent color pastes can be added to this resin. The resin is catalyzed in the same manner as is regular polyester resin.

Buying Polyester Resins

Polyester resins are available in many quantities (pint, quart, gallon, and 5-gallon and 55-gallon drums) in various types of containers. Since the average life of regular polyester laminating and finishing resins, when properly stored in a cool place, is only about six months to a year, it is extremely important that you buy only fresh resin. One way to help assure getting fresh resin is to buy from a volume dealer.

Purchase only the amount of resin that you plan to use in a reasonable amount of time, and store it in a cool place. This is especially important in the case of special-purpose resins, which often have an even shorter shelf life than regular polyester laminating and finishing resins.

Use quality brands. The difference between working with quality resin and a poor grade can be considerable. Quality brands are generally worth the additional cost.

Catalyst for Polyester Resin

The catalyst, methyl ethyl ketone (MEK) peroxide, is sold in various types of containers. These are usually clear plastic so that you can see the amount of catalyst inside. There is a quantity scale marked on the side of the container. Often the container is constructed so that the catalyst can be released by drops. While the amount of catalyst to be added depends on the working temperature, the amount of resin to be catalyzed, and the amount of pot or working time desired (time until the resin starts to gel or set up and is no longer suitable for laminating), it is a small amount in relation to the volume of resin. Usually about 1/2 percent of catalyst by volume will give a working life of about 45 minutes at 70 degrees Fahrenheit. If only a small amount of resin is to be catalyzed, it's extremely important to have an accurate and fast method for measuring and adding a very small amount of catalyst to the resin.

Sometimes sufficient catalyst comes with the resin; in other cases it must be purchased separately. In either case, make certain that you have enough for the temperature conditions in which you will be working.

Styrene

Styrene is a co-active thinner for polyester resin. It's readily available from fiberglass suppliers. Up to 40 percent by volume may be added without harming the stable character of the resin during curing. Thinning, however, is usually necessary only if the resin is to be applied by a spray gun. This is not recommended unless you have the proper safety and protective equipment (see Chapter 4). For most of the laminating and molding projects detailed in this book, spraying resin is not necessary.

Special bubble-inhibitor additives are available that can be used with either polyester or epoxy resin. When added to the resin in recommended amount, bubble formation is suppressed. The additive does not affect the curing of the resin.

Polyester Resin Filler, Putty, and Patching Compounds

A variety of polyester resin filler, putty, and patching compounds are now on the market. Most of these compounds can be used with or without additional reinforcing material. Various materials are used in their manufacture for thickening and strengthening the resin. Polyester resin putties are formulated for special purposes. One type has an additive that will not rust or corrode. Another type is formulated to bond well and be flexible so that it will not crack when hard.

A catalyst is added to these compounds to start the curing or hardening process. Often this is the same liquid catalyst that is used for regular polyester resins, but some polyester resin filling compounds use a paste catalyst.

Most of these compounds have a putty consistency that makes them easy to work with. The manufacturer's directions for adding catalyst and mixing should be followed carefully. Most can be applied with a putty knife, and they will stay in place until they have cured. These generally have some shrinkage, so this must be taken into account in their application.

Acetone

Acetone can be used for cleaning uncured polyester resin from brushes and tools. This must be done before the resin has set up or hardened. Acetone should not, however, be used as a thinning agent for polyester resin. It will evaporate rather than participate in the cure, and cause shrinkage. Even though I have seen acetone widely used for hand cleaning in manufacturing plants, this is definitely not recommended from a health and safety standpoint (see Chapter 4).

Facts on Epoxy Resins

The second main type of plastic resin used for fiberglass laminating and molding work is epoxy which, like polyester resin, is a thermosetting plastic. It is set or cured by heat, which can either be applied chemically from inside the resin, or from outside, or a combination of the two.

The viscosity of epoxy resins, which are produced by the reaction of epichlorohydrin and bisphenal-A, varies from a thin liquid to a thick paste. These have varying molecular weights.

Unlike polyester resins, epoxy resins use a curing agent or hardener—rather than a catalyst—that actually enters into the reaction. The volume of cured epoxy resin will be approximately equal to the combined volume of the epoxy resin and the curing agent or hardener that was added to it.

Compared to polyester resin, epoxy resin has many advantages. It has greater strength and adhesion. Unlike polyester resins, epoxy resins will give strong adhesion to hardwood, metals, and glass. Epoxy resin also has lower shrinkage or curing, an important advantage in some types of molding work. Cured epoxy resin generally has even better chemical resistance than polyester resin.

Epoxy resin also has disadvantages. Epoxy is more expensive, costing at least twice as much as polyester resin. For this reason, epoxy resin is generally used in fiberglass laminating and molding work only when its special properties are required for a particular job. For example, epoxy resin can be used for bonding the first layer of a fiberglass laminate to wood or metal. Once this has cured, additional layers can be added to the laminate with less expensive polyester resin. Epoxy and polyester resins are generally compatible if one is allowed to cure before the application of the other.

Another disadvantage of epoxy resin is that it is generally more difficult to use than polyester resin. Epoxy requires more time and higher temperature for curing. The formulation of modern epoxy resins has been improved to the point where they handle in a manner similar to polyester resins, except for the higher required temperature and longer required curing time. Heat lamps can be used to accelerate the curing of epoxy resin.

Perhaps the biggest disadvantage of epoxy, at least from the point of view of the user, is the potential health hazard. While the cured epoxy resin is innocuous, the epoxy and curing agent or hardener in liquid form are not. Contact with the skin can cause severe dermatitis and other problems. Exposure to the vapors can cause skin irritations, sensitization, and other problems.

When using epoxy resins, it is important that strict health and safety precautions be observed (see Chapter 4). Proper storage of epoxy resins is also important, because there is the potential danger of spontaneous combustion.

Epoxy Resins and Temperature

Epoxy resin comes in two parts, each in a separate container: the basic resin and the curing agent or hardener. The ratio of curing agent or hardener to resin varies depending on the brand and type used. One popular type, for example, uses 4 parts by volume of resin to 1 part by volume of curing agent; another type uses 6 parts by volume of resin to 1 part by volume of hardener; and still another uses a 50-50 mix. The exact amount will depend on the desired pot life and, to a certain extent, on the working temperature.

The best working temperature for epoxy resin is generally about 80 to 85 degrees Fahrenheit, which is higher than the typical 70 to 75 degrees Fahrenheit for polyester resin. While epoxy resin generally has a pot life of 10 minutes to 2 hours, depending on the amount of curing agent or hardener added and other factors, it takes much longer for the resin to cure when applied to a surface. The atmosphere cools the surface, reducing the heat that is generated in the mixture. The amount of hardener that results in a pot life of about 30 minutes gives a curing time of about 20 hours at 70 degrees Fahrenheit when applied to a surface. Application of 150-degree Fahrenheit heat to the surface, such as by using a heat lamp, can reduce the curing time of the same mixture to two to three hours.

Curing Agent and Thinner for Epoxy Resin

A special flexible curing agent is available for use with epoxy resin, which results in a cured plastic that has greater flexibility than when a regular curing agent is used. This is more expensive than regular curing agent or hardener, but ideal for some special laminating and molding applications.

Special epoxy thinner is available that reduces viscosity without decreasing strength or tenacious adhesion. Up to 40 percent by volume may be added without affecting the amount of curing agent to be used or the curing time. A special epoxy solvent is available for cleaning uncured epoxy resin from brushes and tools.

The same color pigments and thixotropic thickening powders described earlier for polyester resins can also be used with epoxy resins. Epoxy resin can be used with any of the fiberglass and nonfiberglass reinforcing materials described earlier in this chapter.

Epoxy Resin Filler, Putty, and Patching Compounds

Many epoxy resin filler, putty, and patching compounds are now on the market. Most of these can be used with or without additional reinforcing materials. Epoxy resin putties are formulated for many uses. There is even a type that will cure under water.

Epoxy putties generally come with the necessary curing agent or hardener. Many types cure rapidly, with a working time of about 10 minutes to an hour, depending on the particular brand, ratio of curing agent or hardener and resin putty compound, and other factors. Because some brands contain metal particles, it's important for some applications that these be of a noncorroding metal alloy.

When selecting epoxy resins and compounds, remember that there are considerable differences in the qualities of various brands. The difference between working with a quality epoxy product and one of poor quality or formulation can be considerable. Quality brands are generally worth the additional cost. Once you find a product that works well for your particular needs, it's best to stick with it.

Unlike polyester resin, epoxy resins can be formulated for use without reinforcing materials as glues, sealers, and paints. Epoxy is well known for its outstanding adhesion and bonding properties.

CORE AND FORMING MATERIALS

There are many core and forming materials that are useful for fiberglass laminating and molding work. These usually become part of the finished fiberglass molding. Molds, discussed later in this chapter, usually do not end up as part of the finished product. The core and forming materials may or may not, in themselves, add structural strength to the fiberglass laminate. Sometimes they serve merely as nonstructural cores for shaping fiberglass stiffeners and other reinforcing members.

Phenolic Microballoons

Phenolic microballoons are microscopic hollow balloons that are combined with either polyester or epoxy resin to form a lightweight material that can be troweled in place. The cells of the phenolic microballoons are filled with nitrogen. The material has a density of about 10 pounds per cubic foot. Even when mixed with resin, the resulting core material will float.

Phenolic microballoons have a flourlike consistency and are red. They are sold in packages by weight and can be purchased in bulk. They are fairly easy to use and form an ideal core material when weight is to be held to a minimum. One disadvantage is the fairly high cost of phenolic microballoons, presently usually over 5 dollars a pound.

Honeycomb Cell Paper

A special honeycomb cell paper is available for fiberglass sandwich construction. It is used to form a honeycomb structure that is light in weight between two layers of fiberglass. The honeycomb cell paper contours to compound curves. It can be useful for some types of fiberglass laminating and molding.

Foamed Plastic

Polystyrene, polyurethane, and polyvinylchloride (PVC) in foamed plastic form are frequently used as core and forming materials in fiberglass laminates and moldings. These foams are available in various densities, with those of from 6 to 8 pounds per cubic foot being most commonly used for fiberglass laminating and molding work. Polystyrene and polyurethane foamed plastics are often used in fiberglass construction of boats, docks, rafts, and other bouyancy items. The foams used for this purpose usually have about 2 pounds per cubic foot density.

Polystyrene foamed plastic is available in precured blocks and sheets in various densities. It is usually less expensive than polyurethane or polyvinylchloride foamed plastic, but is also less resistant to water, decay, and damage from impact. Also, polystyrene is attacked by polyester resins, so it cannot be used as a core or forming material when polyester resins are used. It will work with the more expensive epoxy resins.

Polyurethane foamed plastic is available in precured blocks and sheets in various densities and in foam-in-place liquids, the latter formed by mixing polyol and toluene diisocyanate (TDI) together. The reaction causes the components to foam and cure into polyurethane foamed plastic. Foam-in-place polyurethane is available in pour-in-place and spray-in-place kits. The cure of this foam is sensitive to the ratio of the components, temperature variations, and other factors. Follow the manufacturer's directions carefully when using foam-in-place polyurethane.

Polyurethane foamed plastic is generally more resistant to water, decay, and damage from impact than is polystyrene foamed plastic. Unlike polystyrene foamed plastic, polyurethane can be used with polyester resin. Neither of these plastic materials, once cured to rigid form, can be bent to conform to compound surface curvature. They can be shaped by sawing, filing, and rasping. Foam-in-place polyurethane can be used to fill compartments and cavities of most any shape and size.

Polyurethane foamed plastic is generally more expensive than polystyrene foamed plastic. However, the polyurethane foamed plastic has advantages that frequently make it worth the additional cost for fiberglass laminating and molding work.

Polyvinylchloride (PVC) foamed plastic is a closed cell material that is frequently used as a core in fiberglass sandwich construction (Fig. 2-11). It is available in a thermoplastic form. By application of heat, it can be formed into compound shapes. It can be bent in simple curves at room temperature without breaking down cell structures.

Polyvinylchloride (PVC) foamed plastic is more expensive than polystyrene and polyurethane foamed plastics, but it offers many advantages that are important for certain applications. Because of its closed cell structure, it will not absorb water. It has better chemical resistance than either polystyrene or polyurethane and is non-aging. Polyvinyl chloride foamed plastic will not become brittle, crumble, or deteriorate—common problems with polystyrene and, to a lesser degree, polyurethane foamed plastics. Polyvinyl chloride foamed plastic will accept either polyester

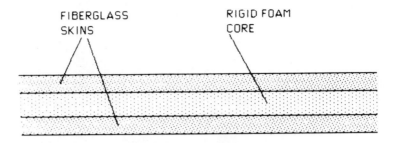

Fig. 2-11. Fiberglass sandwich construction with rigid foam core.

or epoxy resin. It is available in 1/4-, 3/8-, 1/2- and 5/8 inch thick sheets 36 x 72 inches in size.

A popular use of polyvinyl chloride foamed plastic is as a planking material shaped over a male plug. A fiberglass skin is then laminated to the foamed plastic. The male plug is then removed, and the other side of the foamed plastic is sheathed with a fiberglass laminate. The result is a fiberglass laminate with a polyvinyl chloride foamed plastic core in sandwich construction. This generally results in a stronger laminate than if the two fiberglass skins are laminated together into a single unit without the core material.

Wood

Wood has frequently been used over the years as a core and stiffening material for fiberglass constructions. The advantages and disadvantages of using wood for this purpose are frequently debated by fiberglassing experts. The fact that wood and fiberglass have different physical and chemical properties creates many problems when using composite wood and fiberglass constructions.

Thin layers of end-grain balsa are sometimes used as a core material for fiberglass sandwich construction (Fig. 2-12). The end-grain structure is used so that the resin can better penetrate the balsa. End-grain balsa is available for fiberglass construction in the form of thin end-grain blocks held together in sheet form with a gauzelike backing. This allows the balsa to be contoured to complex shapes inside a mold or over a form.

Plywood is frequently used as a structural core material or structural reinforcement for fiberglass decks and superstructures that must

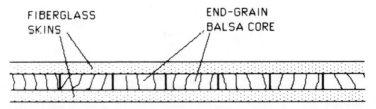

Fig. 2-12. End-grain balsa used as core material for fiberglass sandwich construction.

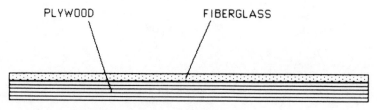

Fig. 2-13. Fiberglass laminate bonded to one side of plywood.

support heavy loads. The plywood is sometimes bonded to the fiberglass on one side only (Fig. 2-13). In other cases, both sides of the plywood are sheathed with fiberglass laminates in a sandwich construction form (Fig. 2-14). Unlike foamed plastic cores, the plywood itself generally adds considerably to the strength and stiffness of the finished laminate.

Only exterior grades of plywood should be used. A common difficulty is bonding the first layer of a fiberglass laminate to the plywood. Since polyester resin does not work well for this, epoxy resin is often used for bonding the first layer of the fiberglass laminate to the plywood. After the epoxy has cured, polyester resin can be used for the remainder of the lay-up. The epoxy resin also provides greater protection from water and moisture getting through to the plywood. If the plywood does become saturated with fresh water, dry rot can become a problem.

Various softwood cores are also used in fiberglass moldings. Although epoxy resin provides greater bonding strength to the wood, the less expensive polyester resin will often suffice. In most cases, fairly substantial fiberglass sheathing laminates are required to fully protect the wood from moisture (and even then some will probably get through eventually) and to keep wood swelling and cracking from damaging the fiberglass laminate surrounding the wood.

The possibility exists for treating the wood with a wood preservative to help prevent dry rot from forming in the wood sheathed in fiberglass. Most wood preservatives make it difficult or impossible to get a good fiberglass bond to the wood, however. They are generally not used when the wood is to be sheathed in fiberglass. Opinions do vary on this point, however, so you might want to do some experimenting to see if you can get an adequate bond for your purposes on wood that has been treated with a preservative.

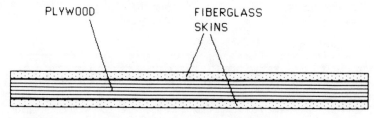

Fig. 2-14. Fiberglass sandwich construction with plywood core.

Various hardwood cores are also used in fiberglass constructions. It is usually more difficult to bond fiberglass laminates to hardwood than to softwood with polyester resin. The more expensive epoxy resin will usually give a good bond. When hardwood is sheathed with fiberglass as a core or structural beam or other member, thick laminates should be used.

When selecting wood for fiberglassing work, make certain it is dry. Techniques for using wood in fiberglass laminating and molding work are covered in later chapters.

Other Possible Core and Forming Materials

The core and forming materials described above are the most commonly used. Other possibilities include metal, ferrocement, and plastics that are compatible with the resin being used. Polyester resin usually does not give adequate bonding strength with these materials; in most cases the more expensive epoxy resin is required.

Sometimes even cardboard and paper are used as core and forming materials. For example, cardboard mailing tubes can be used as a core and form for laminating a fiberglass tube around it.

Careful selection of core and forming materials for the particular project is important. In most cases, plastic core and forming materials are the most compatible with fiberglassing construction. If metal is used, it can bleed rust through the fiberglass laminate. Wood can rot and reduce the strength of the construction. Bonding strength must also be considered. In sandwich construction, for example, the shear strength of the laminate will be greatly reduced if the core material does not bond adequately to the fiberglass skins.

MOLD MATERIALS

A variety of materials, including wood, metal, and many plastics, can be used for making molds. Methodist and materials for making molds are detailed in later chapters.

A manufactured flexible mold compound is frequently used for making molds for craft projects. One type is used by applying mold release agent or a 50 percent solution of Vaseline petroleum jelly and kerosene to the object that a mold is to be made from. Flexible mold compound is then brushed or poured on in successive layers until it is about 1/4 inch thick. The compound cures in about 12 hours. The mold has a hard rubbery texture.

The flexible mold compound is useful for making molds for small items. Larger molds are commonly made from other materials such as fiberglass or wood.

MOLD RELEASE AGENT

A special mold release agent is available. A thin film of mold release is applied to the mold before application of gel coat and lay-up of the fiberglass laminate so that the cured laminate can be removed from the mold without sticking.

PAINT FOR FIBERGLASS

Because of the difficulty in applying gel coat resin to a mold, the finished surfaces are sometimes painted after the molding has been removed from the mold. Two-part epoxy and two-part brushable polyurethane are popular paints for finishing fiberglass. Both bond well and give a tough, durable finish.

OTHER FIBERGLASSING MATERIALS

The materials described earlier are the ones most commonly used for fiberglass laminating and molding work. For some projects, however, additional materials will be required: sealing compounds and bolts, screws, rivets, and other mechanical fasteners, for example. These materials will be described in later chapters along with the techniques for using them.

USE OF MATERIALS

Because materials account for a large part of the cost of fiberglass laminating and molding work when you provide your own labor, careful shopping is important. Buy in sizes and quantities that will result in a minimum of waste. Liquids present special problems. Keep lids tight. Store liquids properly to prevent hardening in containers. Always store polyester resin in cool locations. Heat acts as a catalyst, causing the resin to start hardening. Do not store polyester resin in clear glass or plastic containers for long periods of time, because ultraviolet rays act as a mild catalyst.

QUALITY OF MATERIALS

The best economy is to purchase quality reinforcing materials, resins, and other materials needed for fiberglass laminating and molding projects. Be wary of bargain materials. I've tried some of these, usually with less than satisfactory results.

All reinforcing materials should be clean when you purchase them. Avoid carelessly stored and handled materials. Make certain that resins have been properly stored and are fresh—most have shelf lives of from a few months to about a year. As a general rule, stick to name brands sold by reputable manufacturers.

WHERE TO PURCHASE MATERIALS

It is generally most convenient, though not necessarily least expensive, to purchase fiberglassing materials in the area where you live, provided of course that the stores and supply centers have what you need.

Fiberglassing materials are often sold by paint stores, auto stores, recreational vehicle supply centers, hardware outlets, large discount stores, building suppliers, and marine and boating stores. The selection varies widely. Some areas have stores that specialize in fiberglassing materials and supplies. The one in my area is called TAP Plastics, Inc. They have a large selection of quality fiberglassing materials available at reasonable prices. I've used their products for a variety of fiberglass laminating and molding projects with excellent results. They have stores in many California cities and also in Portland, Oregon, and Salt Lake City, Utah. (For information, write TAP Plastics, Inc., 3011 Alvarado Street, San Leandro, CA 94577.) There are also other fiberglass supply stores in various parts of the United States. Most will give expert advice about fiberglassing and using their products.

I've found that some large paint store chains offer fiberglassing materials at discount prices. I've tried some of these materials. In some cases they were of passable quality; in other cases they were difficult to work with or gave unsatisfactory results. For those who are just starting out in fiberglass laminating and molding, I don't recommend taking a chance with these low-priced products of questionable brands and formulations.

Auto chain and discount stores frequently offer fiberglassing materials intended primarily for auto body repair and customizing. These are usually sold at reasonable prices, and I've had good results with many of these products when used for their intended purposes.

Marine stores frequently stock quality brands of fiberglassing Materials. I've found their prices to be extremely high, with few exceptions. Sometimes the same brands and materials can be purchased in the same area at nonmarine stores at much lower prices.

In my opinion, the best mail-order source for fiberglassing materials and supplies, with one of the largest inventories and selections available anywhere, is Defender Industries, Inc., 255 Main St., New Rochelle, NY 10801. They stock most of the materials described in this chapter, including many of the hard-to-find nonfiberglass reinforcing materials. Their materials are high-quality, name brands, and are sold at discount prices. I've found that even with the cost of shipping, the price is generally much less than if I purchase the materials locally, assuming that I can even find what I need. (See Appendix for other mail order sources for fiberglassing materials and supplies.)

There is a limit to the amount of trouble to which you will want to go for saving money on small quantities of materials. The convenience of purchasing them locally offsets the typically higher prices you will have to pay. For large quantities of materials, it will probably be worth the trouble to shop for the lowest prices.

When I find a brand of a certain material that works well, I try to stick with it. I find, for example, that each brand of polyester resin intended for the same purpose, such as laminating or lay-up, has slightly different handling characteristics. By staying with one brand, I can better learn how to work with it and predict the results.

Chapter 3

Tools, Equipment, and Work Areas

The concern here will be with tools, equipment, supplies and work areas required for making the projects detailed in this book. Only a minimum investment in tools, equipment, and supplies are required to get started. The selection will depend not only on how much you can afford to spend, but also on the kind and number of laminating and molding projects you intend to do. The work area need not be elaborate.

TOOLS, EQUIPMENT, AND SUPPLIES

For our purposes here, tools, equipment, and supplies (other than materials covered in Chapter 2) are grouped together.

Mixing Cans, Cups, Buckets, and Tubs

Containers are required for mixing resins with catalysts or curing agents, for holding solvents for cleaning brushes and tools, and variety of other jobs involved with fiberglass laminating and molding. Clean empty coffee cans will work. Unwaxed paper cups can also be used. Most plastic cups, except those of plastic foam, can be used. Paper, plastic, and metal buckets available at paint stores are fine. For larger laminating and molding jobs, small tubs are convenient for rapid handling of resin, but will not be needed for most of the projects detailed in this book. Usually, only small amounts of resin are mixed (catalyzed) at a time. Short mixing containers with large bases are recommended to keep from accidentally knocking them over and spilling them to a minimum.

Waxed containers should generally be avoided, because the wax can contaminate resin. Sometimes the resin will soften the wax and cause the bottoms to fall out of the containers.

I recommend disposable cans, cups, buckets, and tubs. After a few uses, these can be discarded. It is much more convenient than trying to clean the containers and often less expensive, too. For polyester resin, for example, the acetone required for cleaning a container often costs more than a new disposable container. Clean mixing containers are essential if contamination of resins and other chemicals is to be avoided.

Various fiberglassing workers have their own preferences for mixing containers. For example, some like buckets without handles; others prefer buckets with handles.

Have an adequate supply of mixing containers at hand before you start fiberglass laminating and molding work. Since only a small amount of resin is generally mixed (catalyzed) at a time, the resin usually isn't mixed with catalyst in the container in which it is sold. Once the catalyst or curing agent is added, the resin will harden even if the lid is put back on the container. The resin is generally poured from the container it was purchased in into the mixing container in the desired amount, then the catalyst or curing agent is added.

Mixing Sticks

Wood, plastic, or metal mixing sticks available at paint stores can be used for mixing purposes. Actually, any clean wood sticks of suitable size will do. For most fiberglass laminating and molding jobs, two or more clean sticks will be required. Several lengths of mixing sticks are useful: Small ones about the size of ice cream sticks for mixing resin in small cups, longer and bigger ones to stir resin in gallon cans before pouring out a quantity into another container. Once a stick has been used in catalyzed resin, it should not be used to stir uncatalyzed resin. There is likely to be enough catalyst present to set off the curing reaction.

Paint Brushes

Paint brushes can be used for applying resin to reinforcing materials. I suggest inexpensive (throwaway) brushes, because brushes are quickly ruined by fiberglassing. While solvents are available for cleaning uncured resins from brushes, these will not work on cured resins. Once the resin is allowed to harden in the brush hairs, the brush is finished. Avoid brushes with painted handles. The resin and acetone and epoxy solvents usually cause the paint to come off.

The size of the brushes depends on their intended use. The most useful sizes for common molding work, I believe, are 1/2-, 1-, and 1 1/2-inch-wide brushes. For laminating and molding jobs involving large surface areas, even wider brushes can be used.

Squeegees

Squeegees (Figs. 3-1 and 3-2) with either rubber or plastic blades are useful for scraping off excess resin from reinforcing cloth and woven roving when doing laminating and molding work. This is important for keeping the reinforcing material to resin ratio high for greater strength in the cured laminate. Squeegees can also be used for spreading resin quickly and removing air bubbles.

The blades on some squeegees are stiff. Others have some flexibility (such as those used for cleaning window glass). It will take some experimenting with both types to determine which you prefer for fiberglassing work. Squeegees are available in various widths or in strips that you can cut to desired lengths. Those with blades from about 3 to 6 inches wide are right for most fiberglass laminating and molding work. Some squeegees are gripped by the sides of the blade; others have handles. The choice is largely a matter of individual preference. Those with handles can be useful for getting at hard-to-reach areas.

Scissors or Snips

Scissors or snips are needed for cutting reinforcing materials. These should be sharp and in good working order. Ordinarily, cutting should be done away from wet resin. If you should happen to get resin on scissors or snips, it can be cleaned off with solvent provided that the resin is not allowed to cure. Use acetone for polyester resin and epoxy solvent for epoxy resin.

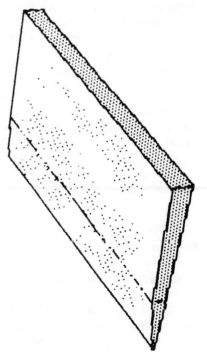

Fig. 3-1. Squeegee without handle.

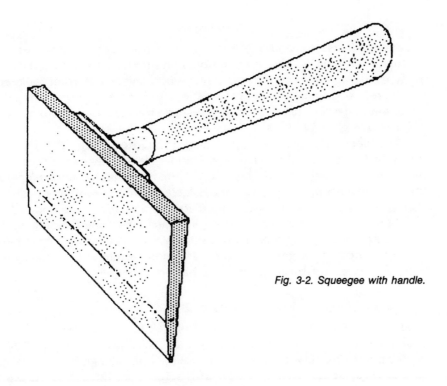

Fig. 3-2. Squeegee with handle.

Masking Tape

Masking tape is useful for many types of fiberglassing repair work. It is a good idea to have several widths on hand such as 1/2-, 3/4-, 1-, and 1 1/2-inch. It will be used for masking off areas.

Protective Paper and Plastic

Construction paper is useful for protecting and masking areas from resin. Plastic drop cloths can be used similarly. However, make certain that they are of a plastic that will not be dissolved by the resin that is being used.

Protecting areas from possible resin splattering, dripping, and spilling is extremely important. Resin, especially if it is allowed to cure, is difficult to clean up from floors and other surfaces.

Rags

You can never get enough rags for fiberglassing work. If you don't have enough of them from old clothes and so on, they can often be purchased at paint stores. They are usually fairly expensive, however. In some areas thrift stores sell them laundered and in bundles.

White rags are best, because resin and solvents can dissolve color dyes. Some synthetics like rayon are not suitable. Paper towels can be used instead of or in addition to rags.

Putty Knives

Putty knives come with a variety of blade widths (Fig. 3-3). I suggest at least two for a start—one with a 1-inch-wide blade and the other with a 2 1/2-inch-wide blade. These are useful for applying resin putties and fillers.

Cellophane

Cellophane is useful for some types of fiberglass laminating and molding work as a release material. It can also be used to seal off the air from small areas when air-inhibited resin is used, so that the surface will cure tack-free.

Utility or Razor Blade Knife

There are many uses for a sharp cutting knife in fiberglass molding and laminating work. A single-edge razor blade can also be used.

Sanding Block

A small block of wood that the sandpaper can be held around (Fig. 3-4), or special sanding blocks that clamp the sandpaper in place (Fig. 3-5) can be used. Sanding blocks are used so that sanding cured fiberglass will not cause the surface to become uneven. This often happens when the sandpaper is held by hand using finger pressure.

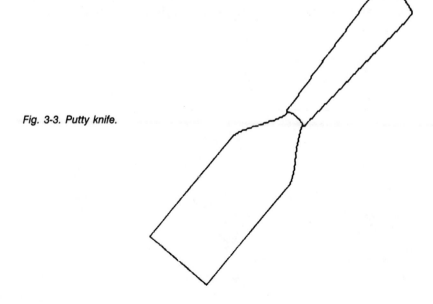

Fig. 3-3. Putty knife.

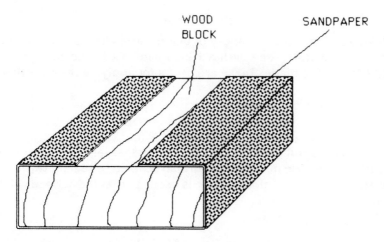

WOOD
BLOCK

SANDPAPER

Fig. 3-4. Sanding block.

Sandpaper or Abrasive Paper

The main types of sanding paper available are garnet, carborundum, aluminum oxide, and silicon carbide—with the aluminum oxide and silicon carbide being the most satisfactory for sanding cured fiberglass. All types can be used, though. Sanding is generally done by beginning with coarser grits and gradually working down to finer grits. Thirty-six grit paper is for very coarse sanding, 150 grit paper is for medium sanding, and 600 grit paper is for very fine sanding.

A selection of grits is needed for fiberglass work. Coarse and medium sanding is usually done with dry sandpaper. Fine sanding is done dry or wet, depending on the particular job, and thus wet/dry sandpaper is recommended for fine grits. Exact selection of sandpaper will depend on the material to be sanded and the particular job at hand, as detailed in later chapters.

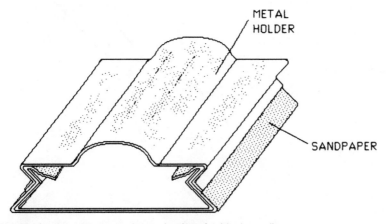

METAL
HOLDER

SANDPAPER

Fig. 3-5. Holder that clamps sandpaper in place for block sanding.

Flat sheets of sandpaper are used for hand and block sanding. Power sanders, if used, require special shapes and sizes.

Surfacing Tools

Surfacing tools come in a variety of shapes, configurations, and sizes. They work well on cured fiberglass, such as after a molding has been removed from a mold. Surfacing tools are especially useful if power grinding and sanding tools are not being used. They make it possible to do fiberglassing work, especially small jobs, without power sanders. These tools raise less dust, making them generally safer to use than power sanders.

Files

Files of various shapes and sizes are useful for fiberglassing work. Usually metal files are used because of the abrasive nature of cured fiberglass. A typical selection for fiberglassing work will include a flat, half round, and round file.

Laminating or Lay-Up Rollers

Laminating or lay-up rollers (Fig. 3-6) are used to remove air bubbles from reinforcing materials that have been impregnated with wet resin. Those with aluminum rollers are generally the most satisfactory. They are easily cleaned with solvent. If resin does harden on the rollers, it can be burned off with a torch. Standard rollers are typically available with 1- and 2-inch diameter rollers from about 3 to 8 inches long. Some feature spiral thread ridges to better break up air bubbles. Special corner rollers (Fig. 3-7) for working in sharp corners of a mold are also available.

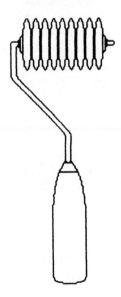

Fig. 3-6. Laminating roller.

Fig. 3-7. Laminating roller for use in corners.

Laminating or lay-up rollers are used extensively for fiberglass lay-up work in a mold. Some have long handles for getting at places that are difficult to reach.

Paint Rollers and Trays

Paint rollers can also be used for applying resin to reinforcing material for lay-up work in a mold. The catalyzed resin can be placed in plastic or metal paint trays for saturation of the roller, which is then rolled over the surface being laminated for application of the resin. This method of applying resin seems inconvenient to me, but some people like it.

Paint rollers are sometimes also used for smoothing the surface of a fiberglass lay-up by placing cellophane or clear plastic food wrap over the wet resin, and then working the paint roller over it. This procedure can save a lot of sanding later. Sanding is difficult and time-consuming work. Manufacturers of fiberglass products try to keep the amount of sanding required to a minimum or to eliminate it entirely in some cases.

Devices for Applying External Heat

These devices for applying external heat can be useful when working with polyester resin in cold conditions. They are almost essential for working with epoxy resin if curing is to take place in a reasonable amount of time. Infrared heat lamps, portable electric heaters, hair dryers, and heat guns can be used. Only flameless heating devices should be used.

Portable Electric Drill and Attachments

Although a limited amount of fiberglass drilling can be done without power tools, they can make the work much easier and faster. If you could choose only one power tool for working on cured fiberglass, it should probably be a portable electric drill. A 1/4-inch electric drill with variable speed will serve many purposes. With metal cutting bits, it can be used for drilling holes in cured fiberglass laminates. With spade-type bits and hole saw attachments, even larger holes can be made.

Abrasive grinding burrs, such as in Fig. 3-8, can be used in the electric drill for a variety of grinding tasks on cured fiberglass.

A disk sanding attachment is useful, especially if you don't have a separate disk sander. Sandpaper in various grits is available to fit the sanding disk attachments. The disk sanding attachments are available in various diameters. The 5-inch and 6-inch sizes are about right for typical fiberglass work. The sanding is usually done with the electric drill turning at a fairly high speed.

Buffing attachments are useful for polishing cured fiberglass. When a variable speed electric drill is used, a slow turning speed is used for polishing and buffing. The principle is high speed for sanding and low speed for buffing and polishing.

Electric drills are mainly designed for drilling holes. They are suitable for limited sanding and buffing work, but for extensive work more specialized sanding and polishing tools are recommended.

Because fiberglass dust is highly abrasive, it can be very hard on power tools. Frequent cleaning of tools with an air gun (attached to an air compressor) will help to protect the tools from wear and damage from this dust. When purchasing tools for fiberglassing work, select those specially designed for use in presence of abrasive dust.

Hacksaw

Hacksaws with metal cutting blades are useful for cutting cured fiberglass. While a regular pistol or saw grip hacksaw frame can be used, a file type handle is often more convenient for cutting fiberglass.

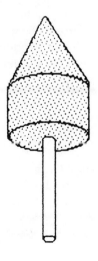

Fig. 3-8. Abrasive grinding burr attachment for portable electric drill.

Saber Saw

Saber saws are useful portable power tools for cutting cured fiberglass laminates. Metal cutting blades should be used.

Portable Power Sanders

The need for power sanders largely depends on the type and amount of molding work that you intend to do. Some molding methods require little or no sanding, others require a great deal of sanding. The three basic types of portable power sanders are: pad or vibrating sander, disk sander, and belt sander.

Pad sanders are available with orbital, straight line, and combination orbital and straight line actions, with the latter being the most useful for sanding fiberglass. Pad sanders are designed for finishing and light sanding.

Disk sanders have disks that are usually mounted at right angles to the drive spindle. This makes sanding much easier that with a disk attachment mounted in an electric drill. Disk sanders are available with disks from about 5 to 9 inches in diameter.

Some disk sanders feature a low speed adjustment that allows them to also be used with buffing and polishing pads. This tool is often called a combination disk sander and polisher. You can use a single tool for two purposes, or you can have separate tools—a high speed disk sander and a low speed disk polisher. The single tool is less costly; two separate tools are more convenient if a large amount of work is to be done.

Belt sanders have a belt of sandpaper that travels over two drums. These are useful for some types of fiberglass sanding work. They can be adjusted for heavy, medium, and light sanding.

Of the three types of sanders, the disk sander is generally the most versatile for fiberglassing work. It also usually takes the most skill and practice to use effectively without leaving undesirable swirls in the surface being sanded. A soft pad between the disk and the sandpaper can be helpful here. Grinding attachments can also be used with many disk sanders. These are sometimes useful for coarse work.

Pad sanders are useful for jobs requiring plenty of finishing sanding. Belt sanders can be used for light, medium, and heavy sanding when greater precision is required than is possible with a disk sander.

Portable Power Polisher

This polisher can be a combination tool with the disk sander, as described earlier, or a separate tool. The polisher should turn at a slower speed than the sander so that heat buildup will not burn the fiberglass surface during buffing and polishing.

Small polishing and buffing jobs can be done by hand with a cloth and necessary compounds. For larger jobs, a portable power polisher can be a good investment.

Compressor

A compressor with an air gun attachment is useful for blowing fiberglass dust from power tools and has many other related uses. It can also be used as an air supply for spray guns. However, I do not recommend spraying resin unless you can afford to invest in very expensive protective equipment, which is beyond the scope of this book.

Methods for applying gel coat and painting fiberglass that don't involve spraying or can be done with spray cans are detailed in later chapters. Brushable two-part polyurethane paint is now frequently used on fiberglass instead of applying a gel coating in the mold.

Spray Gun with Chopper

The spray gun with chopper is a device that sprays catalyzed resin— with the resin, catalyst, and acetone being applied under pressure to the nozzle for spraying. The acetone is for cleaning the nozzle; there is a button for releasing it. The spray gun is combined with a chopper that cuts up fiberglass strands or rovings into short lengths and mixes them with the resin spray. This is a spray-up method for making a fiberglass molding. You spray into a mold to the desired thickness to form the laminate. Laminates produced in this manner are generally weaker than those that are hand laid-up with cloth or woven roving reinforcing material. Nevertheless, this device is widely used in fiberglass manufacturing.

While this device is far too expensive for most do-it-yourselfers and not required for the projects detailed in this book, it is a piece of equipment that you should be aware of. A person going into fiberglass molding as a business will certainly want to consider this tool. It can greatly speed up many types of molding work, and the cost might not be prohibitive if it is spread out over a large number of jobs. Keep in mind that special safety equipment will also be required.

Protective Clothing

Protective clothing is important for health, safety, comfort, and convenience in working with fiberglass and handling, mixing, and applying the related chemicals. The protective clothing should not be thought of as a raincoat, however. Good professional house painters seldom get much paint on themselves or their clothing, while beginners often do. The same applies to fiberglassing work. Whenever you do get resin or other fiberglassing chemicals on yourself or your clothing, you have made a mistake. The protective clothing are there just in case. The clothing should be such that they will protect you from airborne dusts, mists, fumes, and chemicals.

While many types of protective clothing can be worn for fiberglassing, coveralls made from polyolefin fabric seem to work well. They are lightweight, comfortable, and easy to work in. Plus, they offer considerable protection from fiberglass dust and other particles and fiberglassing chemicals. The coveralls should be shaped and fitted so that they will protect the entire body except for the head, hands, and feet.

Boots

While many types of standard work boots can be used, most will be quickly ruined by resins and other fiberglassing chemicals. It is best to set aside a pair just for fiberglassing work. Many fiberglassing workers prefer rubber rain boots, either worn alone or over shoes or boots.

You may use disposable polyethylene boots that are available from paint stores and fiberglassing material suppliers. These will fit over regular shoes or boots and provide good protection from resins and other fiberglassing chemicals.

Gloves

Regular plastic gloves that are resistant to fiberglassing chemicals can be used, but most do not offer enough fingertip sensitivity for fiberglass laminating and lay-up work. Disposable polyethylene gloves are available that do. They may be obtained from paint stores and fiberglassing material suppliers. I recommend these gloves whenever fiberglass reinforcing materials are being handled or used, and whenever fiberglassing chemicals are being handled, poured, mixed, or applied.

Protective Barrier Cream

Special protective barrier cream is available for use on hands. It provides protection from polyester and epoxy resins, hardeners, and caustic and acidic solutions. It is a thick cream that, when applied to skin, gives protection until it wears thin or is washed off. A single application will usually give protection for two or three hours. This protective barrier cream is recommended for hands when protective gloves cannot be worn.

Hand Cleaners, Talcum Powder, and Hand Lotion

While I have observed many fiberglassing workers routinely using acetone for hand cleaning, this practice is definitely not recommended from a health and safety standpoint. Special hand cleaners that will work with or without water are on the market. They will give good results for fiberglassing work without the health and safety hazards associated with using acetone for hand cleaning.

I recommend having soap or powdered hand cleaner and plenty of water handy for frequent hand washing when doing fiberglassing work. Fiberglassing workers frequently apply talcum powder and hand lotion to hands and other skin areas.

Filter Masks and Respirators

Filter or dust masks are available in disposable models and with replaceable filters. These are generally suitable only for nontoxic dusts. The masks are used when sanding fiberglass, but they do not provide protection from fumes given off by fiberglassing chemicals. Filter or dust masks fit over the mouth and nose properly so that dust cannot get in around the edges.

A respirator gives protection against fumes, mists, and dusts from fiberglassing chemicals and other materials. I suggest that you go to a commercial supplier of respirators for industrial use and purchase a good one. Make sure that it is approved for use with the resins and other chemicals you will be using. Get instructions on how to use it and replace cartridges. Purchase extra cartridges and other necessary supplies. I consider a respirator to be an essential piece of equipment—not optional.

The respirator might be somewhat awkward and inconvenient to wear, but the protection that it provides makes it worth the trouble. I have noticed that workers in manufacturing plants tend to take the respirators off when the safety inspectors are not around, but this is just being stupid. While there might not be any apparent immediate effects from breathing the gases or vapors associated with fiberglassing work, there might well be long term effects that will show up later. Why take the chance?

A respirator should first of all provide the necessary protection. Secondary considerations are cost (both of the respirator and of replacement cartridges), comfort, and that the respirator be as lightweight as possible. Carefully follow the manufacturer's directions and instructions for using the particular respirator.

Eye, Face, and Head Protection

Eye, face, and head protection is extremely important for safe fiberglassing work. Many clear plastic eye goggles are available to provide eye protection from nontoxic dusts. Most can be worn with filter masks or respirators that do not cover the eyes.

Face shields are also available, but these are not ordinarily used for most types of fiberglassing work. The shields provide protection from sparks and flying chips, but when used alone they don't provide protection from dusts, such as those from grinding and sanding fiberglass.

Hoods with acetate visors or windows give protection to the head and neck and can be used while wearing some types of respirators. They cover the hair, which is important when fiberglassing overhead (you won't need to do this for the projects detailed in this book).

Advanced Protective and Breathing Equipment

More advanced protective systems that offer complete body protection with piped-in air are sometimes used for industrial fiberglassing work. The high cost of the equipment, not to mention the difficulties involved in operating and maintaining it, generally make it impractical for the do-it-yourselfer.

WORK AREAS

Fiberglass laminating and molding work should ideally be done under laboratory conditions, with controlled temperature, humidity, ventilation, and so on. Often, however, fiberglassing must be done in work areas that are less than ideal.

Some laminating and molding projects can be done on location. For example, a garden pond can be molded where it is to be installed.

Fiberglassing work can be done inside garages and other buildings if there is adequate ventilation, or if fans can be installed. Fiberglassing work can create a mess, so take this into consideration when selecting work areas.

Some fiberglass laminating and molding work can be done outdoors in the open or, better yet, under a patio roof. Working in direct sunlight can have adverse effects on fiberglassing, so it's best to have some type of roof or shield to block the sun.

Sometimes structures are built especially as work areas for doing fiberglass laminating and molding work. This usually isn't practical unless you plan to do considerable work or are going into business.

Chapter 4

Health and Safety

Health and safety in fiberglass laminating and molding work are extremely important considerations. This is also true when working with wood, metal, concrete, and other materials. Each presents certain health and safety hazards and has its own rules of safety. However, fiberglassing is different than many types of work in that it is often more like working in a chemical laboratory than in a shop.

There are two main phases to fiberglass laminating and molding:

● The chemical part of working with liquid resins, adding catalysts or curing agents, mixing them together, applying this mixture to reinforcing material, and so on.
● Working with cured fiberglass after a laminate or molding has been completed—sanding, sawing, drilling holes, bolting two separate moldings together, and so on.

Remember that in the first phase you are dealing with fiberglassing chemicals; in the second you are working with cured fiberglass.

Fiberglass laminating and molding work is generally considered to be reasonably safe for the average person to undertake—if certain health and safety precautions are taken. Anyone who has any reason to believe that he or she might react badly to the chemicals and materials involved should check with a physician before undertaking fiberglassing work.

Anyone who works with fiberglass laminating and molding must learn and practice safe working habits. Most of the materials used in fiberglassing are reasonably safe, but they must be treated with considerable respect. Unfortunately, I've seen many instances where this attitude has not prevailed. Typical examples include not using respirators, smoking while using flammable and even explosive chemicals, and not wearing proper protective clothing.

SAFETY RULES

The basic assumptions are that health and safety are considered important and that safe working habits are worthwhile.

Ventilation

There must be adequate ventilation in the area where you are working. Prolonged and repeated exposures to high concentrations of fumes from resins and other fiberglassing chemicals can result in many health problems. There can also be immediate problems such as skin and eye irritations.

While protective clothing and equipment can reduce these hazards, they should always be in addition to, not as a substitution for, adequate ventilation. When working outdoors, ventilation is rarely a problem. When there is a breeze or wind, always try to work between the direction the wind is coming from and the area where resins and other chemicals are being used. This way fumes are blown away from you and not toward you.

Inside work areas should be open to the outside, preferably on at least two opposite sides, or have a ventilation system. The system should have a fresh air supply and a large exhaust fan capable of changing the room air completely at least once every five minutes, but more often is much better. The exhaust fan must direct the air safely away from the building, not toward a house or other areas where people and other living things are likely to be.

Protective Clothing and Equipment

Wear protective clothing and equipment when handling and using fiberglass reinforcing materials. Fine glass threads and particles from glass fiber reinforcing materials can be irritating to the skin, respiratory system, and eyes. Exposure can result in allergic reactions, skin rash, dermatitis, and other problems. A first step in preventing this is to minimize or eliminate contact between the glass fiber material and the body. Wear the protective clothing and use the protective equipment described in Chapter 3. Do not handle fiberglass reinforcing materials with bare hands. Wear protective gloves such as disposable polyethylene type. This may seem like a needless precaution when, as often happens, the clerk at the store where the material is purchased handles it with his or her bare hands. This careless handling of the material probably adds not only oils to the fiberglass reinforcing material, which makes it more difficult to saturate with resin, but also gives the clerk itchy skin or worse.

The sensitivity to glass fiber reinforcing material varies from individual to individual. Some people handle it constantly without protective equipment and they have little or no discomfort or apparent health problems. However, there may well be long-range problems.

A few people have problems with glass fiber reinforcing material even when they wear the proper protective clothing and equipment. For those with this extreme sensitivity, there are several possible solutions. The first is to quit fiberglassing work. The second is to seek advice from a physician. The third is to use one of the nonfiberglass reinforcing materials such as polyester, polypropylene, or acrylic instead of fiberglass. These nonfiberglass reinforcing materials generally do not cause skin irritation and allergic reactions.

If fiberglass reinforcing materials are used, they can be stored in plastic bags to reduce the amount of glass fiber strands and particles that get into the air. This is especially important in the case of fiberglass mat, where small pieces of glass fiber come off fairly easily.

Special care should be taken when cutting fiberglass reinforcing material, because this also tends to release glass fiber into the air. After cutting, use a vacuum cleaner to pick up any loose strands and particles of glass fiber from the cutting area. The cutting area can be a floor or table. It should be clean and, if desired, covered with plastic or paper, which can be held in place with masking tape. Keep resins and other chemicals away from the cutting area.

Some people don't like to use scissors or shears while wearing gloves. With a little practice, however, scissors or shears can easily be operated while wearing the thin, disposable type polyethylene gloves, which give good fingertip sensitivity.

If, despite all precautions, glass fibers do get on the skin, a cold shower followed by application of hand lotion often helps relieve itching. If skin rash or any other unusual reactions develop, a physician should be consulted.

Wear protective clothing and equipment when sanding fiberglass. Sanding cured fiberglass produces a fine dust that can cause respiratory, eye, and skin problems. Wearing proper protective clothing and equipment while sanding fiberglass is extremely important. A well-fitted filter mask or respirator and eye goggles or protective hood are especially important. The protection of skin, including hands, should not be overlooked.

Even hand sanding can raise considerable dust. Hand sanding with or without a block can usually be done while wearing polyethylene disposable gloves.

Power sanding presents even greater dust problems. Even bearings and brushes in power tools tend to suffer the effects, so the importance of not breathing the dust or getting it in your eyes or even on your skin is obvious. One problem is operating power sanders while wearing gloves. With a little practice this can generally be done, even though fairly substantial gloves are generally required. The thin disposable polyethylene type wear through quickly. Rubber and plastic gloves with liners work satisfactorily. Chemical resistance is not a critical factor here; the sanding is done on cured fiberglass.

When sanding laminates where nonfiberglass reinforcing materials were used, the effects of dust contact with skin are generally less severe than when glass fiber reinforcing materials are used in the laminate.

Sanding dust that is allowed to accumulate in the work area can cause problems, because some of it can easily become airborne. Frequent cleaning of the work area with a shop-type vacuum cleaner will help to alleviate this problem.

If any respiratory, eye, or skin problems should develop, consult a physician. This should rarely be necessary provided that the safety precautions for sanding fiberglass are observed, especially the use of proper protective clothing and equipment.

Avoid breathing chemical fumes. This applies to individual chemicals and the chemicals after they have been mixed, such as catalyst or curing agent added to resin. Again, wear a well-fitted respirator that is safety approved for the particular chemicals you are using. In order for the respirator to remain effective, the cartridges or elements should be changed as directed by the respirator's manufacturer. In addition, keep chemicals as far away from your face as possible. This is an extremely important safety rule—one that too often isn't given the attention it deserves. While some breathing of fumes from resins and other fiberglassing chemicals is almost inevitable in fiberglass laminating and molding work, it should be kept to an absolute minimum.

Avoid eye contact with chemicals. The consequence of splattering or otherwise getting even small quantities of these chemicals in the eyes can be extremely serious. This must be avoided. The first line of prevention is careful handling, pouring, mixing, and application of the chemicals. The second line of defense is to always wear goggles when using these chemicals. Finally, always know the emergency steps to be taken if any of the chemicals being used do contact the eyes. This varies depending on the particular chemical. Sometimes the eyes must be flushed with large quantities of water, and emergency medical treatment is needed as soon as possible. The specific instructions should be on the label of the product's container.

Avoid skin contact by wearing protective clothing and using protective equipment to keep the fiberglassing chemicals from getting on your skin. Take care when handling, pouring, mixing, and applying the chemicals.

Some of the chemicals are potentially more dangerous than others. Be especially careful of methyl-ethyl-ketone (MEK) peroxide catalyst for polyester resins and epoxy resins and curing agents, which can produce chemical burns if they come into direct contact with the skin. Even polyester resin, generally considered to be much safer to use than epoxy, can cause skin irritations, dermatitis, and other health problems from skin contact.

Manufacturer's Recommendations

Always read the labels on fiberglassing resins and other products not only to learn how to use them, but also to learn what safety precautions should be followed. Follow directions carefully and observe all health and safety precautions. Often the steps to be taken in case of an accident—for example, if resin gets in the eyes—are given. Always know what these are before you use the product, just in case.

Fire Danger

Keep resins, catalysts, curing agents, solvents, and other fiberglassing chemicals away from fire and flame. Most polyester resins are flammable in both liquid and cured states. Even fire-retardant polyester resin is flammable when in liquid state. The same applies to epoxy resins and epoxy curing agents or hardeners. Appropriate warnings should be on containers' labels. Because spontaneous combustion is a possibility, these chemicals should be properly stored. Heat from fire or flame can cause catalysts for polyester resins to explode. Acetone and epoxy solvents are both highly flammable. They give off heavy vapors that tend to travel close to the floor. If the solvents reach fire or flame, they will explode. A spark can cause the same thing to happen. These solvents should be handled with the same care and caution as gasoline. Proper storage also increases shelf life.

Avoid Open Flame Heaters

Do not use open flame heaters in fiberglassing work areas. This is an extremely important consideration. If the work area is to be heated, make certain that the heater used does not create a fire and explosion hazard with the chemicals and materials being used. The same applies to heating devices used for speeding cure of resins. When selecting and installing heaters for use in fiberglassing work areas, get professional advice.

No Smoking

Do not smoke in fiberglassing work areas, especially when resins and other chemicals are being used. This might seem obvious, but I think it should be mentioned. Some people don't take the obvious seriously. If you must smoke, take a break from the fiberglassing work and do it away from the work area, especially away from the resins, solvents, and other chemicals.

Other Rules

● Never mix a polyester accelerator like cobalt napthenate directly with a catalyst such as methyl-ethyl-ketone (MEK) peroxide. An explosion can occur. Most manufactured polyester resins already have the necessary accelerator mixed in at the factory. If you do add an accelerator, it should first be added to and mixed with uncatalyzed resin before adding the catalyst.

● Methyl-ethyl-ketone (MEK) peroxide should not be stored in metal containers, because spontaneous explosions can occur as a result of prolonged contact with metal. This catalyst usually comes in plastic containers. Do not put this catalyst in metal containers for storage.

● If you do get resins or other fiberglassing chemicals on your skin, remove them as soon as possible. Use a rag to wipe them off. Use soap or hand cleaner and water to wash them off—the sooner, the better. Problems from skin contact with chemicals depend, among other things, on the particular chemical, the amount, and the length of exposure.

● Develop good working habits. Keep the work area clean and organized. Discard floor and bench covers, disposable containers, and similar items when they are no longer serviceable. Clean up spilled chemicals. Clean working habits make fiberglass laminating and molding work safer and more enjoyable, as do good lighting and comfortable temperatures.

● Keep visitors away from the work area. Don't allow other people without protective clothing and equipment to be in the work area. Keep children and pets away from work area.

● Follow all safety precautions and use proper safety equipment when using power tools. Always follow safe operating procedures for portable electric drills, saber saws, sanders, and other tools used for fiberglassing work. This is the nonchemical part of fiberglassing. Don't get careless.

● Have one or more approved fire extingishers handy in the work area, in case of a fire emergency. These should be of a type that will work on chemical fires.

● Keep a first aid kit handy. This kit is a good idea for almost any type of shop work. Minor cuts, blisters, and so on should be treated to prevent possible infection.

● If you work alone, have assistance nearby.

DEVELOPING SAFE WORKING HABITS

Knowing the rules of safety is one thing; practicing them is quite another. Do-it-yourselfers can usually follow or disobey safety rules as they please. A fiberglassing worker employed in a manufacturing plant generally is not given this choice. Using safety equipment and following safety rules, including those that apply to the worker's own health, are part of the job. Allowing workers to violate safety rules and precautions can result in heavy fines.

The prudent do-it-yourself fiberglassers develop safe working habits because they want to. The basic idea is to follow the rules of safety right from the start. In this way they will soon become habit. Safety rules will become a routine part of fiberglassing, and you won't have to consciously think about them. The breathing respirator and gloves automatically go on for a job that calls for them, and so on.

On the other hand, not following safety rules and precautions can become habit, too. You will only be working with the chemicals for a few minutes, so you don't bother with the respirator. Nothing much seems to happen. Next time you do an even longer job without the respirator. This practice continues until working *without* the respirator becomes habit. This, of course, is to be avoided. Don't take chances.

Finally, don't let the requirements for safe fiberglassing scare you out of doing your own fiberglass laminating and molding work. The safety precautions that should be taken are not excessive, they are just less familiar. Fiberglass laminating and molding can be a safe and rewarding experience.

Chapter 5

Techniques
for Laminating
and Molding Fiberglass

A variety of molding methods can be used for laminating fiberglass reinforced plastics to desired shapes. The two basic types are contact and pressure molding, with many variations of each. It is important to differentiate the two, because they will be referred to throughout the book.

CONTACT MOLDING

Contact molding is a fiberglass lay-up in or over a male or female mold or form that uses no outside pressure on the side of the laminate away from the mold or form surface. We will begin with an introductory project using contact molding before going on to more complicated contact mold forms. This introductory project will also introduce the basics of fiberglass laminating.

Introductory Contact Molding Project

One type of simple contact mold is a flat mold, which is a smooth, flat surface used for laying up a fiberglass laminate. The surface that is against the flat mold will be the finished side of the molding. This method of molding gives only one smooth side to the laminate. The introductory project is to mold a 10- x -10-inch flat square of fiberglass that can be used as a decorative pad on a tabletop or for other similar purposes.

Making the Mold. The first step is to make the mold, which is a

10-x-10-inch square of 1/2-inch plywood. The decorative pad could, of course, be a larger or smaller size by changing the mold size, but the 10-x-10-inch size is ideal for a first project. Mark the plywood and cut it to a 10-x-10-inch square (Fig. 5-1).

Because the surface of the plywood will be used to mold the surface of the molding, it must be smooth and prepared so that the molding will not stick.

While various methods can be used to make the wood surface suitable, a method frequently used is to apply a thin layer of polyester resin to the surface, allow this to cure, and then sand and buff the surface until it is very smooth. If you have never before used polyester resin, this will also allow for catalyzing and applying polyester resin without having to worry about reinforcing material on your first attempt.

Catalyzing Polyester Resins. The curing process for polyester resins is called *polymerization*. It is fully initiated when a catalyst, usually methyl-ethyl-ketone (MEK) peroxide, is added. The amount of catalyst to be added depends mainly on the working temperature, the amount of resin to be catalyzed, and the working life desired. With a typical polyester resin, 1/2 percent of catalyst by volume will give a working life or gel time (the time the catalyst is added until it achieves a gelatinous consistency) of about 60 minutes at 75 degrees Fahrenheit. The working life or gel time is also called pot life. It's the time you have for applying the resin. After the resin has started to gel, the remainder in the pot or container should be discarded. If applied to reinforcing material, it will result in a lumpy mess. The resin usually becomes hard soon after this, although the complete cure goes on for two weeks or more. Catalyzed polyester resin will actually cure faster in the container in which it is mixed than when spread thin (as when applied to reinforcing material).

It is important to note that different brands and types of polyester resins will not all cure at the same rate when the same amount of catalyst is added. Follow the catalyzing directions for the particular polyester resin being used. This might vary somewhat from the amounts given in this chapter, which are intended only as a general guide.

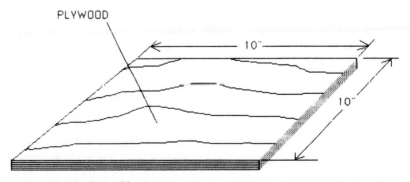

Fig. 5-1. Plywood for flat mold.

In the previous example, if the amount of catalyst is doubled to 1 percent of catalyst by volume, the pot life would be reduced to about 30 minutes at the same 75 degrees Fahrenheit working temperature. Two percent of catalyst by volume would further reduce the pot life to about 15 minutes.

If the working temperature in these examples is 90 degrees Fahrenheit and the same amounts of catalyst are added, the pot life in each case would be approximately cut in half. It would reduce to about 30 minutes with 1/2 percent of catalyst by volume added, to about 15 minutes with 1 percent of catalyst by volume, and to about 7 1/2 minutes with 2 percent of catalyst by volume.

If the working temperature in these examples is 60 degrees Fahrenheit and the same amounts of catalyst are added, the pot life in each case would be approximately doubled. It would increase to about 2 hours with 1/2 percent of catalyst, to about 1 hour with 1 percent, and to about 30 minutes with 2 percent.

When first starting fiberglass laminating and molding work, small quantities of resin, usually from about 1 to 8 ounces (1/2 pint), will be catalyzed for use at a time. If larger quantities are used, there is danger of the pot life expiring before all of the resin can be applied. Because high heat buildup can occur with resin in a container, it is best to pour the resin out in a safe place on the ground. Allow it to harden before discarding it in a trash can.

As experience is gained, you may be able to catalyze and use larger amounts of resin at a time for some types of laminating and molding work. In fact, if you were to attempt a large molding project, say a swimming pool, you would never get finished catalyzing such small amounts of resin at a time. However, for learning purposes, start with small amounts and then gradually work up to larger amounts as your skill and confidence improve.

You will need a method for adding small quantities of catalyst. For most laminating and molding work, the amount of catalyst added will range from about 1/2 to 4 percent by volume. Often the catalyst is supplied in dispensers that allow release of the catalyst by drops. I recommend that this type be used. In order to catalyze 1 ounce of resin with 1 percent by volume of catalyst, about 4 drops would be required. The containers also usually have a scale marked on them. The markings are generally in ounces or cubic centimeters. Two hundred drops, for example, equals about 1/6 ounce or 5 cubic centimeters of catalyst.

I find it most convenient to add the catalyst by counting drops when small amounts of resin are to be catalyzed. Most catalyst dispensers allow adding drops quickly, so 100 or more drops can be added in a short time period. If you intend to do a lot of fiberglassing, you will probably want to invest in a special catalyst dispenser that allows for more rapid dispensing. These are available from fiberglassing suppliers. The catalyst can be purchased in large containers and then poured into the special dispenser as needed. If the catalyst that comes with the resin you purchase does not come in a "drop" dispenser, you can use a regular eye dropper.

For the introductory contact molding project, only small amounts of resin will be catalyzed at a time. This can be applied quickly, so only a short pot life is required. Usually 2 to 3 percent catalyst by volume is used.

One ounce of resin is 1/16 pint. One-half percent by volume of catalyst is about 2 drops; 1 percent is about 4 drops; 2 percent is about 8 drops; and 3 percent is about 12 drops. At 75 degrees Fahrenheit, the 1/2 percent would give a pot life of approximately 60 minutes. One percent would give approximately 30 minutes. Two percent would give about 15 minutes. Three percent would reduce the pot life or working time to about 7 1/2 minutes, which would usually still allow more than enough time for applying this small amount of resin.

Using the same mixtures, higher working temperatures reduce the pot life and increase the curing rate. Lower working temperatures increase the pot life and decrease the curing rate.

The general principle is: the more catalyst, the faster the curing time—the less catalyst, the slower the curing time. Also, the higher the temperature, the faster the curing time—the lower the temperature, the slower the curing time. With most polyester resins, the same pot life and curing time can be maintained in a range of temperatures—usually from about 60 to 90 degrees Fahrenheit—by varying the amount of catalyst used.

If at all possible, try to do your first practice project with a working temperature as close to 75 degrees Fahrenheit as possible. The idea is to keep the temperature constant at first so that you can better concentrate on other factors. After you have a little practice, you can learn to fiberglass in various temperatures.

Before continuing with the introductory project, it is a good idea to first practice catalyzing polyester resin to become familiar with the effects of adding different amounts of catalyst to equal amounts of resin on gel and curing time, especially if you have never before worked with polyester resins. This will also give you an opportunity to study the characteristics of cured polyester resin without reinforcing material. You need either finishing or general-purpose polyester resin, catalyst for the resin, four mixing cups (the kind sold at drug stores with ounce markings on the sides, four small mixing sticks, and one longer mixing stick that can be used to stir the resin in the container in which it was purchased. You need a piece of wax paper, in addition to paper to protect the area where you will be working, which can be on a bench, floor, or concrete surface outside. Again, remember to use proper protective clothing and safety equipment, as detailed in Chapter 3, and follow the safety rules explained in Chapter 4.

You also need a clock positioned so that it can be seen from the work area, and a pencil and notebook for recording the results of your practice work for future reference. Have a thermometer in the work area so you will know what the working temperature is at any given time. You can start by writing the temperature down in your notebook.

When you have everything ready, open the container that the resin came in. Carefully stir it with a clean stirring stick. When removing the stick from the container, allow as much of the resin to drain off the stick back into the container as possible. Use a clean rag to clean off the remaining resin from the stick. Put the stick aside for later use. Keep this one stick for use only for stirring uncatalyzed resin in the containers in which it is sold.

Pour 1 ounce of resin into each of the four cups. The markings on the sides of the cups can be used as a guide, or you can use a 1-ounce measuring scoop such as the kind used in the kitchen (but don't use it for kitchen duty again). Replace the lid on the resin container and set it aside.

To one of the cups containing 1 ounce of resin, add 2 drops of catalyst. Stir with one of the small sticks. Wait about 30 seconds. Observe the time on the clock and write this down in your notebook. Pour the catalyzed resin out on the piece of wax paper and spread it into a thin layer with the mixing stick. Use the small stirring stick to poke at the resin as the curing takes place. Because 2 drops of catalyst added to 1 ounce of resin is only about 1/2 percent by volume, it should take about an hour for the resin to gel. It should reach a cheeselike consistency and become hard. By using the stick as a probe, follow the process of the liquid changing to a solid. Write down how long it took from the time the catalyst was added until the gel state was reached, and then how much longer it took for the resin to become hard. The results depend on many factors such as the particular resin and catalyst used, the working temperature, and the humidity. Almost certainly the gel time and curing time were much longer than really necessary. It would be very inefficient to use such a slow curing time if you want to get any volume of work done that depends on the cure of the first resin before the next layer can be applied.

With a second cup containing 1 ounce of resin, add 4 drops of catalyst or twice as much as was added to the first batch. This is about 1 percent by volume of catalyst. Again, mark down the starting time, noting the percentage of catalyst added, and observe the time to gel state and until the resin becomes hard. These times should be about half as long as previously. The resin should be poured from the cup to an area of the wax paper separate from the first (now hard) resin, which should be saved for later experimenting. Also, keep track of the percentage of catalyst that was added to each one.

Use the stirring stick to spread the resin out on the wax paper into a thin layer. This should be done so that the resin will still be in one piece when it hardens. Use the stick as a probe to determine when the gel state is reached and when the resin becomes hard.

With the third cup of 1 ounce of resin, repeat the same practice exercise, except this time add 8 drops of catalyst. This is approximately 2 percent by volume. Mark down the starting time. Stir. Wait about 30 seconds, then pour the resin out on the wax paper in an area away from the first two batches of resin, which should now be hard. Observe and record the time to gel and to when the resin becomes hard. For a typical polyester resin, the time to gel should be about 15 minutes, but your results might vary. It should become hard very soon—faster than when less catalyst was used.

With the last cup containing 1 ounce of resin, repeat the same steps, except this time add 12 drops of catalyst. This is about 3 percent by volume of catalyst. It should take only about 7 1/2 minutes for the resin to reach the gel state. The resin should become hard very quickly. Record the times in your notebook. Your results should be similar, but not necessarily exactly the same, as mine (Table 5-1).

This will probably be enough fiberglassing for one practice session. Save the four pieces of cured resin. Mark them so that you can remember how much catalyst was added to each one. These pieces of cured resin will be used later to study the characteristics of resin without reinforcing material. Finish the practice session by cleaning up the work area and putting everything away in an organized manner. Remember to store resin in a cool, dry place.

Data kept in your notebook will be useful as a reference for future fiberglassing. For example, if you later want to catalyze 4 ounces of the same resin, the amount of catalyst to be added for various working times can be determined. For instance (using my data), 16 drops of catalyst are used (4 x 4) for a 30-minute gel—or working-time. Remember, however, that the data is for a specific working temperature (my working temperature in this practice exercise was 75 degrees Fahrenheit). If you do future work at a different working temperature than you had for your test data, this will have to be taken into consideration, as detailed previously in this chapter.

Cured Polyester Resin Without Reinforcing Material. Polyester resin alone, without reinforcing material, is quite brittle when cured. Take the piece of resin that was formed by 1/2 percent by volume of catalyst and

Table 5-1. Catalyzing Polyester Resins.

Amount of Resin (Ounces)	Percent by Volume of catalyst	Drops of Catalyst	Minutes to Gel	Minutes until Hard
1	1/2	2	50	70
1	1	4	30	35
1	2	8	15	17
1	3	12	7 1/2	8

place it on a hard surface. Tap it with a hammer. It will probably shatter rather easily. Repeat with the other three pieces of cured resin. Could you observe any differences between the ease (or difficulty) of shattering them? In most cases you probably would not be able to detect any differences. The variations in the amounts of catalyst used for this practice exercise probably would not have much effect on the strength of the cured resin. The situation might be different, however, if you went to greater extremes, such as less than 1/2 percent catalyst by volume or more than about 5 percent catalyst by volume. Too little catalyst would also give an unreasonably long working time, and too much catalyst would not give you enough time to apply the resin to anything.

You just found out that the resin without reinforcing material will shatter easily, but you also ruined the material in the process. It is very difficult to tell the strength of a laminate without harming the laminate, but destructive testing can tell you plenty about the strength and integrity of your fiberglass laminates. This is the advantage of practice work.

Coating Plywood Mold with Polyester Resin. The next step in the introductory contact molding project with a flat mold is to coat the plywood mold with a thin layer of polyester resin. In addition to the 1/2-inch-thick plywood cut previously to a 10-inch square, you will need either finishing or general-purpose polyester resin, catalyst for the resin, a mixing cup, a small mixing stick, one longer mixing stick, and a small paint brush for applying the resin. You will also need a piece of paper to protect your working area.

Two strips of wood of equal height should be placed under the plywood mold, which is positioned with the mold surface upward. Stir the resin.

Pour 1 ounce of resin into the mixing cup. Replace the lid on the resin container and set it aside. If available, add about 1/8 ounce of styrene monomer to the resin and mix thoroughly. While the resin can be applied to the plywood surface without this, the thinning action of the styrene will serve to thin the resin and allow it to better penetrate the surface of the wood.

Add 8 drops of catalyst to the ounce of resin. This is approximately 2 percent by volume, which should give about 15 minutes of working time. Wait about 30 seconds, then brush a smooth thin layer of the catalyzed resin onto the mold surface of the plywood (Fig. 5-2). When you have finished applying the coat of resin to the plywood, clean the paint brush. Allow the resin to harden on the plywood surface. Even though this should happen about 15 minutes after the resin is applied, it is best to wait at least an hour before attempting to sand the surface.

Lightly sand the surface with fine-grit paper to remove the surfacing agent. This is not necessary if laminating resin is used. An alternate method is to remove the surfacing agent by wiping the surface with acetone on a rag.

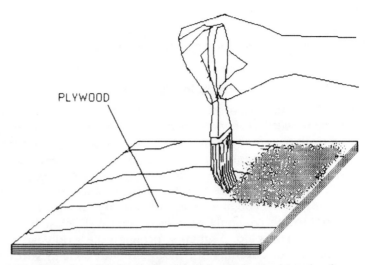

PLYWOOD

Fig. 5-2. A thin layer of catalyzed polyester resin is brushed onto plywood surface.

Apply a second coat of polyester resin in the same manner as detailed above. When this has cured, apply a third coat in the same manner. When the third coat has cured, sand with fine-grit wet/dry sandpaper and water using a sanding block.

Polish the surface using a buffing compound. This can be done by hand with a clean cloth, or with a power buffer.

It is important to take the necessary time to make a good mold. Any defects in the mold surface will be copied on the moldings made with the mold.

This completes the construction of a flat mold for the introductory contact molding project.

MATERIALS AND INSTRUCTIONS

From here on, the materials on the list below will be used repeatedly for the projects in this chapter. Following the materials list is a set of general instructions which will be applied to the rest of the projects in this chapter. Be sure to note that any variation from the basic instructions are listed.

Materials List

1. A paste-type mold release.
2. Polyester gel coat resin.
3. Laminating and/or finishing or general-purpose polyester resin.
4. Catalyst for the resin.
5. Mixing cups (with ounce markings on the side).
6. Small mixing sticks.
7. One longer mixing stick to stir the resin.
8. One small paintbrush for applying the resin.

9. Fiberglass cloth, mat, or woven roving.
10. A piece of paper to protect the working area.
11. Proper safety equipment (see Chapter 3).

Basic Instructions

Step 1. Place the plywood molds on the protective paper with the mold surface upward. Apply a coat of the paste-type mold release, using a clean cloth to spread a thin layer of the release over the entire mold surface, including the edges. The purpose of this is to keep the molding from sticking so that it can be removed after it has cured.

Step 2. Apply the gel coat on the mold surface over the mold release (Fig. 5-3). When you have everything ready, begin by opening the container that the gel coat polyester resin came in. This can be clear resin or any desired color; color pigments formulated for polyester gel coat resin can be added. Carefully stir the resin with a clean stirring stick. When removing the stick from the container, allow as much of the resin to drain off the stick back into the container as possible. Use a clean rag to clean off the remaining resin from the stick. Put the stick aside for later use. Keep this one stick for use only for stirring uncatalyzed gel coat resin in the containers in which it is sold.

Step 3. Pour the gel coat resin into a mixing cup. The markings on the side of the cup can be used as a guide, or you can use a 1-ounce measuring scoop such as the kind used in the kitchen (but don't use it for kitchen duty again). Replace the lid on the gel coat resin container and set it aside.

Step 4. Add the drops of catalyst to the resin. This will be approximately 2 percent by volume for these instructions, which is the percentage usually used for polyester gel coat resin at 75 degrees Fahrenheit. However, this might vary for the particular brand of gel coat resin being used. Follow the manufacturer's directions. Wait about 30 seconds, then brush a smooth thin layer of the catalyzed gel coat resin onto the mold surface of the plywood. The gel coat should have a thickness of only .02 to .03 inch. A thicker layer will be brittle and subject to cracking and crazing. When you have finished applying the coat of resin to the plywood, clean the paint brush with acetone. This must be done before the resin hardens if the brush is to be used again. Allow the resin to harden.

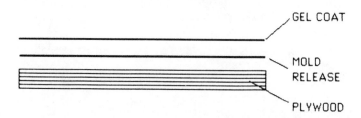

Fig. 5-3. A thin layer of gel coat resin is applied over the mold release agent.

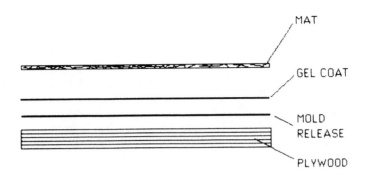

Fig. 5-4. A layer of mat is applied over the gel coat.

Gel coat resin usually doesn't contain a wax additive so that the laminate can be laid up directly over this with no additional surface preparation.

Step 5. The first layer of fiberglass cloth (or mat, or woven roving) reinforcing material is now laminated to the gel coat (Fig. 5-4). When using cloth as an example—because 1 square yard of 10-ounce cloth weighs approximately 10 ounces, the approximate amount of resin required to saturate or wet out the reinforcing material can be calculated. Cloth laminates are typically 45 to 50 percent fiberglass cloth reinforcing material and 50 to 55 percent resin by weight (while mat laminates are 25 to 35 percent fiberglass reinforcing material and 65 to 75 percent resin). So, for a 50 percent cloth ratio, the weight of the resin should be equal to the weight of the cloth. A 12-inch square is 1/9 of a square yard, which weighs slightly less than 1 ounce. Thus, you will need approximately 1 ounce of resin to saturate the cloth in this example. (These measurements will change throughout the chapter.)

Step 6. Pour the resin into a mixing cup. You will need about 7 1/2 minutes of working time to apply the resin. Always look in your notebook and see how much catalyst you should add. For a working temperature of 75 degrees Fahrenheit, this should be about 12 drops for 1 ounce of resin.

Step 7. Add the drops of catalyst to the resin and stir. Wait about 30 seconds. Then, using the paint brush, apply a coat of resin over the gel coat layer that was laminated to the mold surface previously.

Step 8. Position the fiberglass cloth (mat, woven roving) over the wet resin so it is centered and press it down and smooth it out. The brush can be used for this. With mat, use a pressing or dabbing action. Avoid using a brushing action because this can lump the mat up. You won't have this problem with cloth or woven roving, so a brushing action can be used, but be careful not to unravel the cut edges of the cloth (or woven roving).

Step 9. Saturate the cloth (mat, woven roving) with resin. Spread the resin as evenly as possible (Fig. 5-5). All areas should be saturated, including the inch that sticks out past the mold all the way around. When

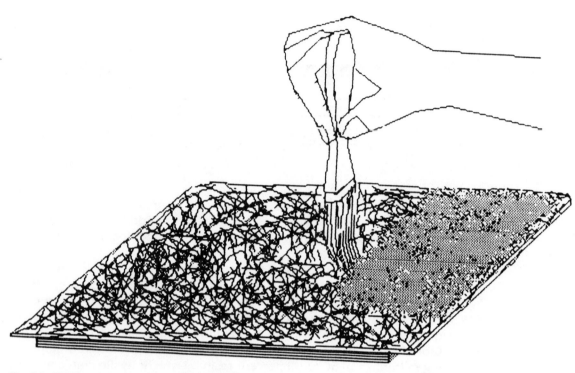

Fig. 5-5. The fiberglass mat is saturated with resin.

everything looks alright, clean the resin from the brush with acetone.

On the first attempts at laminating, it usually works best if you allow one layer to harden before applying the next layer. Later, you will be able to apply two or more layers at a time.

Step 10. The next step is to add the second layer of cloth (mat, woven roving) reinforcing material to the laminate (Fig. 5-6). Pour resin into a mixing cup, add catalyst to resin and stir. Wait about 30 seconds and, using a paintbrush, apply a coat of resin over the first layer of cloth (mat, woven roving).

Step 11. Position the fiberglass cloth (mat, woven roving) over the wet resin so it is centered and press it down and smooth it out. The brush can be used for this, but be careful with mat, as described in Step 8.

Step 12. Saturate the cloth (mat, woven roving) with resin. Spread the resin as evenly as possible. All areas should be saturated, including the inch that sticks out past the mold all the way around. When everything looks alright, clean the resin from the brush with acetone before the resin hardens.

Step 13. Allow the laminate to thoroughly cure and remove it from the mold. Even though the mold release was used, it still might be necessary to pry the laminate loose with a putty knife or other similar tool.

Step 14. This completes the chemical part of the construction. Mark the pattern for the 10-inch square on the fiberglass molding and saw off excess laminate (about an inch all the way around). Sawing methods are detailed later in this chapter.

Step 15. Next, file and sand the edges smooth, rounding the edges slightly.

Step 16. Polish and buff the gel coat surface and edges of the laminate. When appropriate, you can cut a piece of felt to a 9 1/2-x-9 1/2-inch size and cement it to the bottom side of the laminate (the side that wasn't against the mold) to protect the tabletop or other surface where the pad is used.

Step 17. In a similar manner, a cloth (mat, woven roving) laminate can be made with three or more layers of mat reinforcing material. A three-layer cloth laminate for example, should be approximately 1/20 inch thick, about the same as a single layer mat laminate made with 1 1/2-ounce mat. The three-layer cloth laminate will be stronger (assuming that the laminate was laid up properly and quality materials were used). It takes approximately three times as long to lay up the cloth laminate, since three layers of reinforcing material are required instead of one. The cloth laminate contains more fiberglass reinforcing material and less resin.

Molding the Pad. To mold the pad, you will need the items on the materials list. You will use a piece of 1 1/2-ounce fiberglass mat 12 x 12 inches square, and a piece of 10-ounce fiberglass cloth 12 x 12 inches square.

Now refer to the basic instructions Steps 1 through 13.

In Step 5, remember that 1 square foot of 1 1/2-ounce mat weighs about 1 1/2 ounces—the approximate amount of resin required to saturate or wet out the reinforcing material. Mat laminates are 25 to 35 percent fiberglass reinforcing material and 65 to 75 percent resin by weight. For a 25 percent mat ratio, triple the weight of the mat in resin is required to fully wet out the mat. One and one-half ounces multiplied by three is 4 1/2 ounces. To be certain you will have enough resin, 5 ounces can be used.

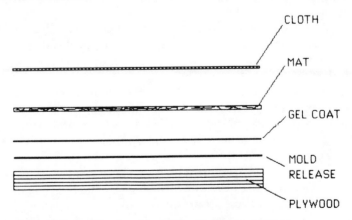

Fig. 5-6. A layer of cloth reinforcing material is added to the laminate.

In Step 6, use 5 ounces of resin.

In Step 7, add 60 drops of catalyst.

In Step 10, 1 square yard of 10-ounce cloth weighs approximately 10 ounces, so the amount of resin required to saturate or wet out the reinforcing material can be calculated. Cloth laminates are 45 to 50 percent fiberglass cloth reinforcing material and 50 to 55 percent resin by weight. For a 50 percent cloth ratio, the weight of the resin should be equal to the weight of the cloth. A 12-inch square is 1/9 of a square yard, which weighs slightly less than 1 ounce. Thus, you will need approximately 1 ounce of resin to saturate the cloth.

At this stage of the introductory project, you have moved from chemical construction to working with cured fiberglass.

Using Tools on Cured Fiberglass

For many laminating and molding projects, there is additional work to be done after the laminate has been removed from the mold. Frequently required operations include drilling, sawing, filing, and sanding. Before returning to the introductory project, let's first take a look at these tasks.

Drilling: It is generally easy to drill holes in fiberglass. While a hand drill can be used, a portable electric drill makes the work much easier. Metal twist drills or bits are commonly used for making small holes. For slightly larger holes, spade-type bits can be used. These are convenient for holes from about 3/8 inch up to about 2 inches. You must have a different bit for each desired hole size. Even larger holes can be made with hole saws. These often come in sets with blades for holes from about 3/4 inch up to about 3 inches. A different blade is used for each desired hole size. Spade bits and hole saws can be used in portable electric drills.

Before drilling, carefully mark the desired location for the hole. While a laminate can be drilled from either side, it's best to drill with the bit starting on the gel coat side (Fig. 5-7). If you drill from the reverse side, there is considerable danger of chipping the gel coat beyond the hole area when the twist drill, spade bit, or hole saw blade goes through the laminate.

A center punch or other sharp-pointed object is used to make a small indentation or pilot mark for centering the point of the drill or bit. Do this carefully so as not to chip the gel coat beyond the area where the hole is to be located.

Center the point of the drill or bit in the small indentation or pilot mark. Angle drill as desired and drill a hole through the fiberglass. When using a hole saw, if you can get to both sides of the laminate, drill halfway through. Finish the drilling from the opposite side using the same pilot bit hole.

For larger holes, if you require a hole size between two sizes of spade bits or hole saws, drill the hole one size smaller. File the hole out to the desired size. Filing is covered later in this chapter.

If scrap pieces of fiberglass are available, practice drilling various

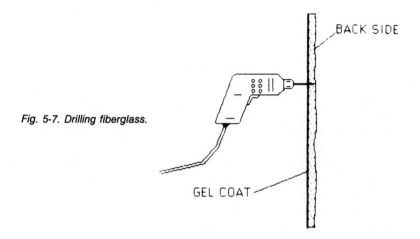

Fig. 5-7. Drilling fiberglass.

BACK SIDE

GEL COAT

sizes of holes through them. Try to make clean holes with no chipping of resin around the hole.

Sawing: There are many situations in fiberglass laminating and molding work where sawing of cured fiberglass laminates is required. You can saw by hand with a hacksaw or coping saw with a fine-tooth metal-cutting blade, or you can use a portable power saber saw with a fine-tooth metal cutting blade.

Whenever possible, do your sawing from the gel coat side (Fig. 5-8). This will help to prevent chipping of the gel coat. It is sometimes helpful to place masking tape over the fiberglass on the gel coat side in the area where the cut is to be made. Sawing lines can be marked on the masking tape with a pencil. The pattern should be carefully marked. When making critical cuts, leave a little extra and then use a file to take it to final size.

Cutouts and holes larger than available drill and hole saw sizes are usually made by sawing. Begin by carefully marking the pattern. Drill a pilot hole for starting the saber saw blade. Saw around the pattern line. When completing the cutout, hold the cutout piece of fiberglass so that it will not break off. This might cause chipping of the gel coat.

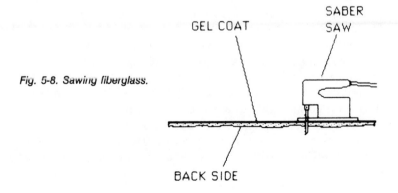

Fig. 5-8. Sawing fiberglass.

GEL COAT

SABER SAW

BACK SIDE

If the cutout or hole must be an exact size, make it slightly smaller and then file to final size.

If scrap pieces of fiberglass are available, practice making both straight and curved cuts. For cutting, clamp small pieces between two pieces of wood in a vise.

Filing: Metal files can be used for filing fiberglass. The filing is generally done on edges of laminates. Whenever possible, position yourself on the gel coat side of the fiberglass laminate (Fig. 5-9). File from side to side or apply pressure on the forward stroke only, lifting the file off the work when drawing it back. These methods will help prevent chipping the gel coat. Edges can be filed flat or rounded. If the file notches become clogged with fiberglass, clean them with a file brush or solvent.

If scrap pieces of cured fiberglass are available, practice filing both straight and rounded edges on the laminates.

Sanding: Surfacing tools can be used for coarse work on edges and surfaces of fiberglass laminates. These tools come in many shapes and sizes. They are extremely useful for fiberglass work, especially if power sanders are not used. A large amount of material can be removed quickly.

The blades tend to clog and dull rather quickly, so frequent cleaning of the blades with solvent and replacement of dull blades are necessary. The blades on surfacing tools cannot ordinarily be resharpened; they must be replaced when they become dull or break. Replacement blades are readily available for most sizes and shapes of surfacing tools.

Observe safety precautions given in Chapter 4 for sanding fiberglass. A filter mask or respirator, eye protection, and protective clothing should be worn.

Aluminum oxide or silicon carbide sandpaper or abrasive paper can be used for sanding fiberglass. The general principle in sanding fiberglass is to start with the coarsest grit required for the particular job and then work down to finer grits. Coarse and medium sanding of fiberglass is generally done dry. Fine sanding is often done wet. Sandpaper with a waterproof adhesive is used. The paper is dipped in water, which keeps the grit from clogging while sanding. This keeps scratching to a minimum.

Coarser grits of sandpaper remove the most material, but also leave the deepest scratches. Medium grits will remove these scratches and leave smaller scratches. Finer grits leave even smaller scratches, which will be filled in when the surface is painted—or polished out in the case of gel coat surfaces. Take care when using coarse grits of sandpaper to avoid making scratches that extend below the desired finished surfaces. Otherwise, these will have to be filled in with fiberglass putty or other surfacing compound to achieve a smooth finish.

The sandpaper can be folded and held between the thumb and fingers, but this method is generally used only for very fine sanding. When used with coarser sandpaper, it can result in an uneven wavy surface.

66

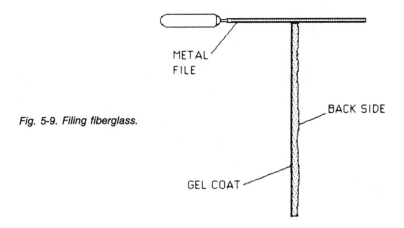

Fig. 5-9. Filing fiberglass.

METAL FILE

BACK SIDE

GEL COAT

Most hand sanding is done with a block. Use a small block of wood with or without a foam rubber pad, with the sandpaper folded around it. Special blocks or flexible holders have a clamping arrangement for holding the paper in place. Block sanding allows the removal of high spots without affecting adjacent low areas.

While small areas of fiberglass can be easily sanded by hand, power sanders are almost indispensable for larger areas. Disk sanders are generally the most useful all-around type for fiberglass. These usually have turning speeds of about 5,000 revolutions per minute. A large amount of material can be removed with a minimum amount of effort.

It takes practice to learn how to use a disk sander. When improperly used, the surface can be gouged. In most cases the sanding disk is held nearly flat to the surface, light pressure is applied, and the disk is kept moving. The disk sander is also used for feathering edges by holding the sanding disk at a slight angle to the surface. Anyone who plans to do a lot of fiberglass sanding should take the time and trouble to learn to use a disk sander properly.

Belt sanders are useful for some types of fiberglass sanding work, especially for sanding large flat areas. Like disk sanders, they can be used to remove a lot of material quickly and to smooth out uneven surfaces. They can also be adjusted for fine sanding. Again, it takes practice to avoid over-sanding. This is especially true on curved surfaces; belt sanders are generally not recommended for such areas.

Pad or finishing sanders are frequently called "vibrator" sanders. These sanders won't take much material off, so they are generally only suitable for finishing sanding and other light tasks. They are the easiest type for a beginner to use because gouging the surface is seldom a problem.

These sanders are available with straightline (back and forth), orbital, and combination actions. While all three types can be used on fiberglass, the orbital and combination types are generally preferred.

When using a pad sander, apply only light pressure and keep the pad moving. Excessive pressure can cause the shaft to break off on the sander, especially on light-duty types.

Other tools and jobs: Grinding tools, such as an abrasive grinding burr used in an electric drill, can be used on fiberglass. For small projects such as models, hobby grinding and sanding tools can be used similarly.

Power buffers are frequently used to polish fiberglass gel coats. Buffers should turn at about 2,500 revolutions per minute, about half the speed of a typical disk sander, to prevent the pad from heating up to the point where it can burn the fiberglass. Higher speed causes more heat to build up.

Fiberglass cannot be bent by hammering or other means. Hammering will only shatter the resin in the laminate. Even heating will not soften the laminate so that it can be bent, although enough heat will cause the resin in the laminate to burn. Fiberglass does have a certain amount of flexibility, but this allows only slight bending. Generally, fiberglass is molded to the desired shape and is not bent or forced into any other shape after it has cured and is removed from the mold.

Finishing the Introductory Project. The above techniques are used to finish the introductory project. First mark the pattern for the 10-inch square and saw off excess laminate (about an inch all the way around.) File and sand the edges smooth. Round the edges slightly, as shown in Fig. 5-10.

Polish and buff the gel coat surface and edges of the laminate. Cut a piece of felt to a 9 1/2- x -9 1/2-inch size and cement it to the bottom side of the laminate (the side that wasn't against the mold) to protect the tabletop or other surface where the pad is used. This completes the introductory flat contact molding project.

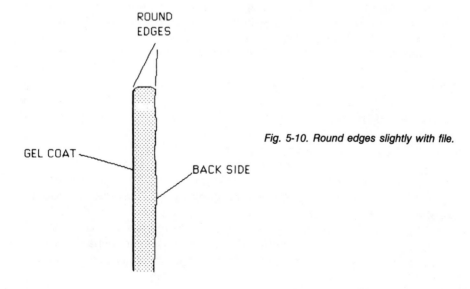

ROUND
EDGES

GEL COAT

BACK SIDE

Fig. 5-10. Round edges slightly with file.

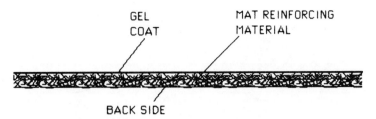

Fig. 5-11. Single-layer mat laminate.

Other Laminates Using the Same Contact Mold

The same flat contact mold can be used for a variety of laminates. By making these laminates, you can learn the fundamentals of contact molding on a simple flat mold before going on to more complicated molds.

Single Layer Mat Laminate. To mold the single layer mat laminate (Fig. 5-11), you will need the same mold used for the introductory project, plus the items on the materials list. For this project, you need a piece of 1 1/2-ounce fiberglass mat 12-x-12 inches square.

Now follow the basic instructions, Steps 1 through 9.

In Step 5, 1 square foot of 1 1/2-ounce mat weighs approximately 1 1/2 ounces, so the approximate amount of resin required to saturate or wet out the reinforcing material can be calculated. Mat laminates are typically 25 to 35 percent fiberglass reinforcing material and 65 to 75 percent resin by weight. For a 25 percent mat ratio, triple the weight of the mat in resin is required to fully wet out the mat. One and one-half ounces multiplied by 3 is 4 1/2 ounces. To allow for some waste, use 5 ounces.

In Step 6, for a working temperature of 75 degrees Fahrenheit, the amount of catalyst should be about 12 drops for 1 ounce of resin or 60 drops for 5 ounces.

After completing Step 9, allow the laminate to thoroughly cure. Then remove it from the mold. Even though the mold release was used, it still might be necessary to pry the laminate loose with a putty knife or other similar tool.

This completes the chemical part of the construction. Mark the pattern for the 10-inch square on the fiberglass molding and saw off excess laminate (about an inch all the way around). File and sand the edges smooth, rounding the edges slightly.

Polish and buff the gel coat surface and edges of the laminate. Cut a piece of felt to a 9 1/2-x-9 1/2-inch size and cement it to the bottom side of the laminate (the side that wasn't against the mold) to protect the tabletop or other surface where the pad is used.

Single Layer Cloth Laminate. To mold the single layer cloth laminate (Fig. 5-12), you will need the same mold used for the introductory project, a piece of fiberglass woven roving 12 × 12 inches square, plus the items on the materials list.

Now follow the basic instructions, beginning with Step 1.

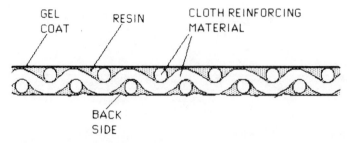

Fig. 5-12. Single-layer cloth laminate.

In Step 5, cloth laminates are typically 45 to 50 percent fiberglass cloth reinforcing material and 50 to 55 percent resin by weight. For a 50 percent cloth ratio, the weight of the resin should be equal to the weight of the cloth. A 12-inch square is 1/9 of a square yard, which weighs slightly less than 1 ounce. Thus, you will need approximately 1 ounce of resin to saturate the cloth.

In Step 6, use 1 ounce of resin and 12 drops of catalyst.

Single Layer Woven Roving Laminate. To mold the single layer woven roving laminate (Fig. 5-13), you will need the same mold used for the introductory project, plus the items on the materials list. For this project, you will use a piece of 24-ounce fiberglass woven roving 12 × 12 inches square.

Now follow the basic instructions, Steps 1 through 18.

In Step 5, because 1 square yard of 24 ounce woven roving weighs approximately 24 ounces, the approximate amount of resin required to saturate or wet out the reinforcing material can be calculated. Woven roving laminates are typically 40 to 45 percent fiberglass woven roving reinforcing material and 55 to 60 percent resin by weight. Thus, the weight of the resin will be slightly more than the weight of the woven roving. A 12-inch square is 1/9 of a square yard, which weighs approximately 2.7 ounces (calculated as 24 divided by 9). Thus, you will need approximately 3 ounces of resin to saturate the woven roving.

In Step 6, use 3 ounces of resin. For a working temperature of 75 degrees Fahrenheit, the amount of catalyst should be about 12 drops for 1 ounce of resin or 36 drops for the 3 ounces of resin.

After Step 9, skip to Step 15 and proceed to Step 18.

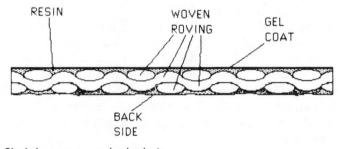

Fig. 5-13. Single-layer woven roving laminate.

COMPARING THE MAT,
CLOTH, AND WOVEN ROVING LAMINATES

The mat, cloth, and woven roving reinforcing materials result in laminates with different characteristics. Probably the most notable difference is that the laminates have different thicknesses. The mat laminate is approximately 1/20 of an inch thick, the cloth 1/64, and the woven roving 1/25. The weight of the reinforcing material before the laminates were trimmed is approximately 1.5 ounces for the mat, 1.2 for the cloth, and 2.7 for the woven roving. The weight of the resin, not including the gel coating (which is approximately 1 ounce for each laminate), is approximately 4.6 ounces for the mat laminate, 1.2 ounces for the cloth laminate, and 2.8 ounces for the woven roving. The total weight of the finished laminates before trimming—including the gel coat layer—is about 7.1 ounces for the mat laminate, 3.4 ounces for the cloth, and 6.5 ounces for the woven roving.

Remember that the resulting laminates have different thicknesses.To produce laminates that are all approximately 3/32 inches thick, it takes two layers of 1 1/2-ounce mat, six layers of 10-ounce cloth, and 2.3 layers of 24-ounce woven roving.

While the total cost of the resin and reinforcing material for the various laminates of the same thickness will vary depending on factors such as where and how you purchase your materials, a mat laminate will generally be cheapest. The cost will be about 25 percent more for a woven roving laminate, and the cloth laminate will cost about twice as much as the woven roving. The mat uses slightly more resin, followed by cloth, and then woven roving. However, it's mainly the cost of the reinforcing materials that will make the difference. Mat is the cheapest. Cloth is generally about four times as expensive as mat. Woven roving is about half the cost of the cloth, or about 80 percent higher than mat. Remember that these figures are for the same total thickness of laminate.

Why not just always use mat and save money? Whenever mat will serve the purpose, this is the economical way to go. Cloth and woven roving have important strength advantages over mat, however, that outweigh the cost disadvantages for some applications.

Two-Layer Mat Laminate. Two layers of the same reinforcing material can be laminated together. To mold a two-layer mat laminate (Fig. 5-14), you will need the same mold used for the introductory project, two pieces of 1 1/2-ounce fiberglass mat 12 × 12 inches square, plus the items on the materials list.

Now follow the basic instructions, Steps 1 through 16.

In Step 5, because 1 square foot of 1 1/2-ounce mat weighs 1 1/2 ounces, the approximate amount of resin required to saturate or wet out the reinforcing material can be calculated. Mat laminates are typically 25 to 35 percent fiberglass reinforcing material and 65 to 75 percent resin by weight. For a 25 percent mat ratio, about triple the weight of the mat in resin is required to fully wet out the mat. One and one-half ounces multiplied by 3 is 4 1/2 ounces. To allow for some waste and to be certain you will have enough resin, 5 ounces can be used.

In Step 6, you see by consulting your notebook that the amount of catalyst is 12 drops for 1 ounce of resin or 60 drops for 5 ounces.

In Step 7, remember to avoid a brushing action, since it might lump up the mat.

In Step 10, you will be using 5 ounces of resin and adding 60 drops of catalyst.

In Step 16 remember: a mat laminate can be made with three or more layers of mat reinforcing material. A three-layer laminate should be approximately 1/8 inch thick. Compare this with the two-layer laminate, which should be about 3/32 inch thick and the single-layer laminate, which should be about 1/20 inch thick.

Two-layer Cloth Laminate. To mold a two-layer cloth laminate (Fig. 5-15), you will need the same mold used for the introductory project, two pieces of 10-ounce fiberglass cloth 12 × 12 inches square, plus the items on the materials list.

Now follow the basic instructions, Steps 1 through 16.

In Step 5, remember that 1 square yard of 10-ounce cloth weighs approximately 10 ounces, so the amount of resin required to saturate or wet out the reinforcing material can be calculated. Cloth laminates are typically 45 to 50 percent fiberglass cloth reinforcing material and 50 to 55 percent resin by weight. For a 50 percent cloth ratio, the weight

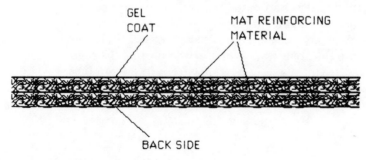

Fig. 5-14. Two-layer mat laminate.

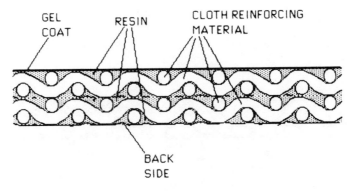

Fig. 5-15. Two-layer cloth laminate.

of the resin should be equal to the weight of the cloth. A 12-inch square is 1/9 of a square yard, which weighs slightly less than 1 ounce. Thus, you will need approximately 1 ounce of resin to saturate the cloth.

Two-layer Woven Roving Laminate. To mold the two-layer woven roving laminate (Fig. 5-16), you will need the same mold used for the introductory project, two pieces of 24-ounce fiberglass woven roving 12 × 12 inches square, and the items on the materials list.

Now follow the basic instructions, Steps 1 through 16.

In Step 5, because 1 square yard of 24-ounce woven roving weighs approximately 24 ounces, the amount of resin required to saturate or wet out the reinforcing material can be calculated. Woven roving laminates are typically 40 to 45 percent fiberglass woven roving reinforcing material and 55 to 60 percent resin by weight. Thus, the weight of the resin will be slightly more than the weight of the woven roving. A 12-inch square is 1/9 of a square yard, which weighs approximately 2.7 ounces (calculated as 24 divided by 9). Thus, you will need approximately 3 ounces of resin to saturate the woven roving.

In Step 6, use 12 drops of catalyst for 1 ounce of resin, or 36 drops for 3 ounces of resin. So in Step 7, add 36 drops of catalyst to the resin and stir.

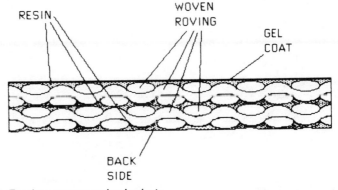

Fig. 5-16. Two-layer woven roving laminate.

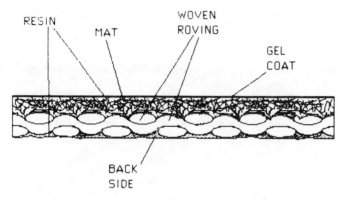

Fig. 5-17. Mat and woven roving laminate.

In Step 10, again use 3 ounces of resin, adding 36 drops of catalyst.

In Step 16, remember: a woven roving laminate can be made with three or more layers of woven roving reinforcing material. A three-layer laminate is about 1/8 inch thick, slightly thinner than a three layer mat laminate using 1 1/2 ounce mat. A three-layer woven roving laminate is much stronger (assuming that the laminate was laid up properly and quality materials were used). Woven roving also builds up thickness quickly and is only slightly more expensive on a laminate thickness basis than mat. Woven roving is a fairly difficult material to work with, however. For laminating work, a layer of mat is generally sandwiched between layers of woven roving to help fill in the coarse weave pattern so that resin-rich areas will not be present.

Laminating with More Than One Kind of Reinforcing Material. In a similar manner laminates can be laid up with more than one kind of reinforcing material. The first introductory project was an example with one layer of mat laminated to one layer of cloth. Mat is also frequently used with woven roving to fill in the coarse weave pattern of the woven roving and give a better bond between layers (Fig. 5-17). In some cases, mat, cloth, and woven roving is used in the same laminate (Fig. 5-18).

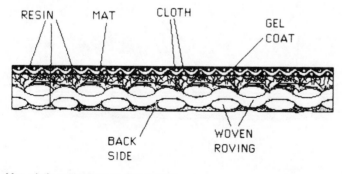

Fig. 5-18. Mat, cloth, and woven roving laminate.

74

Contact Molding Methods

The above contact molding projects with a flat mold serve as an introduction to contact molding. Contact molding is a fiberglass lay-up in or over a male or female mold or form without pressure being applied to the side of the laminate away from the mold or form surface—that is, other than the contact pressure. Contact molding can be done by hand lay-up, with the resins applied to the mold surface by brush, rollers, and/or squeegees; or spray up, with the resins and reinforcing material sprayed from a chopper gun; or some combination of the two methods.

Advantages of contact molding over pressure molding (covered later in this chapter) are that molds and other equipment are generally less expensive, less experience is required to do the lay-up work, and large fiberglass structures can be molded that would be impractical using pressure molding.

A main disadvantage of contact molding is that the back side of the laminate is not as smooth and fair as the side against the mold, because there is no way to mold or form the back side during the cure of the laminate. Other disadvantages are that contact molding is slower, involves hand labor, and is somewhat less accurate when small parts with complicated shapes are required.

When contact molding is used in manufacturing, the side of the laminate that is to be smooth and finished almost always goes against the mold surface. The mold for a bathtub (Fig. 5-19) is almost the reverse of that of a toy car body (Fig. 5-20). In each case the desired finished side is the side that will be against the surface of the mold and is applied first in the laminating process. This is usually the case regardless of whether a resin gel coat is to be applied inside or over the mold as the first layer of the laminate, or to be painted later. Manufacturers want to avoid sanding, which involves plenty of labor even when power sand-

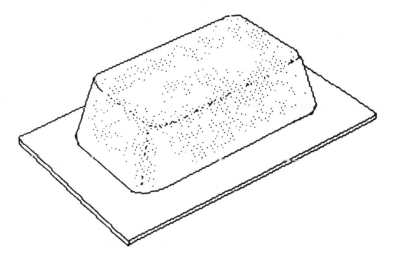

Fig. 5-19. Contact mold for bathtub.

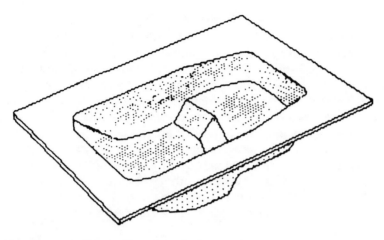

Fig. 5-20. Contact mold for making toy car body.

ing equipment is used. Imagine, for example, the sanding that would be necessary if the bathtub or swimming pool were molded in reverse. The rough side would be the side that needs to be smooth. Even if all the sanding necessary to achieve this were done, it would be difficult to obtain the surface possible from contact with a mold. Also, each molding would be slightly different on the finished side from the previous one. The gel coat layer would have to be sprayed on last, like paint, instead of against the mold first. This would not matter, of course, if the molding is to be painted rather than gel coated.

Manufacturers have developed methods for avoiding sanding and fairing of large areas of fiberglass when contact molding is used. For example, an ice box can be molded in two sections—one for the outside and one for the inside. Insulation material is placed between the two layers and the layers are bonded together (Fig. 5-21).

Some do-it-yourselfers use a one-off (only one is made) construction method that does involve sanding and fairing. This can be done over a low-cost form (Fig. 5-22), thus avoiding the expensive cost of tooling a mold. A lot of sanding and fairing is required, however, and even then it is difficult to achieve the smooth and fair surface comparable to that possible from a quality mold.

Male and Female Molds. There is considerable confusion in the way the terms "male" and "female" molds are used. Usually, if the surface of the laminate that is to be the "outside" finished surface goes on first against the mold, it is considered as a female mold. The toy car body mold shown in Fig. 5-20 is easy to recognize as a female mold, but this is not the case with the "female" mold for the bathtub shown in Fig. 5-19, which by appearance looks like a plug or male mold.

As mentioned previously, most manufacturing using contact molding is done with, by the above definition, female molds. We will follow this definition of a female mold here, but it should be pointed out that

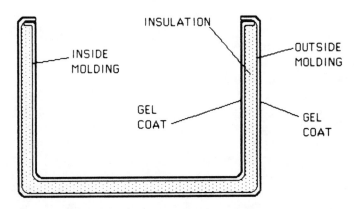

Fig. 5-21. Ice box molded in two sections so that both inside and outside have finished gel coat surfaces.

some fiberglassers and writers of fiberglassing material use some other definition of female and male molds.

It costs a lot of money to make a quality female mold. Once the mold is made, however, hundreds of fairly accurate duplicates of the same molding can be made from the same mold. The mold is used for the lay-up of one laminate or molding, which is then removed from the mold. The same mold is then used to lay up a second molding. While there are limits—molds do wear out and/or become damaged eventually—it is not unusual for 100 or even 1,000 moldings to be made from a single mold. When a new mold is required, a molding from the original can be used to make a plug to mold a new mold (more on this later).

Before a female mold is constructed, the usual procedure is to have a design made up (either on paper or as a small scale model) of what the finished molding is to look like. This is not the only way, however. Many fiberglass molds have been taken from existing car bodies, boats, swimming pools, bathtubs, and so on, including from those made out of materials other than fiberglass. There might be some problems involved here. The design for a specific item made out of wood, metal, or concrete may not be the best design for fiberglass construction. Still,

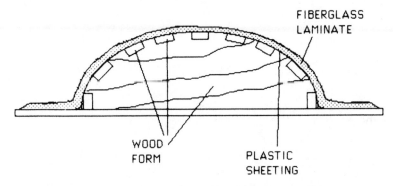

Fig. 5-22. One-off molding over form requires sanding and fairing finished surface.

successful molds have been "designed" in this manner. This is often an ideal method for the do-it-yourselfer, as detailed in later chapters. Essentially, you duplicate an existing object in fiberglass.

Making a Plug. A plug is constructed to the design lines in the shape of the finished surface desired for the fiberglass molding. A plug for a bathtub is shown in Fig. 5-23. Notice that is looks like a bathtub. A plug for a toy car body is shown in Fig. 5-24. Notice that it looks like a toy car body. The idea is to duplicate these shapes. Notice also that an existing bathtub or toy car body could also be used as a plug.

The plugs can be made from wood, plaster of paris, clay, concrete, various plastics, or a combination of materials. The plug must be as close as possible to the design lines or desired shape of the finished molding, because a mold will be taken from the plug to duplicate its shape. Any unevenness or lack of fairness in the plug will be transferred to the mold, and in turn to fiberglass laminates made from the mold. While it is possible to make some changes in the mold itself after it has been made, this is extremely difficult. It is generally much easier to get the plug exactly the way it should be, so changes will not have to be attempted on the mold itself. On the plug, you are working with the shape for the finished laminate. On the mold, you are working with the shape surrounding the laminate that is to be molded. Shaping the plug is usually much easier.

Making a Mold From a Plug. Once the plug is finished, the next step is to make a mold from the plug. This might seem like the long way to go about the job. Why not skip the plug and just construct the mold in the first place? With simple shapes this can sometimes be done, but with more complicated shapes it is very difficult to make a mold that is accurate, smooth, and fair in this manner. You would be working with the shape of the area surrounding the desired object, and with complicated shapes this involves a difficult change in thinking.

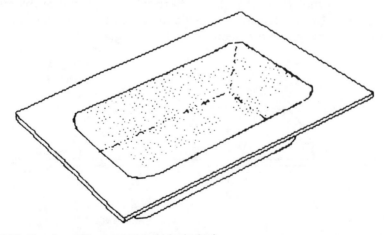

Fig. 5-23. Plug for making contact mold for bathtub.

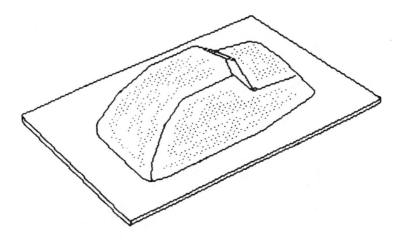

Fig. 5-24. Plug for toy car body.

Molds can be made from a variety of materials, but a fiberglass lay-up, while somewhat expensive, seems to work best for most uses, especially if a large number of moldings are to be made from the mold. Essentially, a fiberglass laminate is laid up over the plug. Remember, however, that the term "plug" is being used to mean shapes like a plug (the toy car body, for example), flat surfaces, and pan shapes (the bathtub, for example).

First, the plug is sprayed or otherwise coated with a wax releasing agent or polyvinyl alcohol (PVA) parting agent. The plug can thus be removed from the fiberglass mold once the lay-up has been completed and it has cured. While methods vary, a typical one is to first wax the plug, buff this out, and then spray on a layer of PVA.

A special color gel coat called tooling gel coat is applied. A color is selected that will contrast sharply with the gel coat color of the items to be molded later. Tooling gel coat is a special tough gel coat formulated for use on molds. For do-it-yourself mold making, regular gel coat will often give satisfactory results.

The tooling gel coat is allowed to harden. A layer of fiberglass mat usually follows. Polyester resin is used in most cases. The mat layer is usually used first to give the mold a smooth surface. The weave pattern of cloth and especially woven roving will frequently show through on the surface if the mat layer is not used first.

The laminate is then followed by layers of desired reinforcing material. Frequently, layers of mat are alternated with woven roving to make the mold stiff and strong. The mold must be constructed so that it will not flex or sag when a laminate is laid up in it. For larger molds, additional reinforcing is frequently required. This may be from materials like metal and wood. The reinforcing often acts as a base for wheels, so the mold can be moved about the work area, and as a frame so the mold can be turned to desired angles for lay-up work.

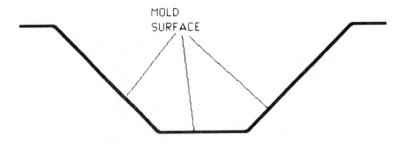

Fig. 5-25. Contact mold without undercuts.

The mold can be in one piece if there are no undercuts. Figure 5-25 shows a mold without undercuts and Fig. 5-26 shows one with undercuts, which would not allow removal of a laminate from the mold. The mold with undercuts could be removed from the plug by destroying the plug, but this still would not solve the problem of later removal of a molding from the mold.

If undercuts are present, the mold can be made in two or more pieces, which are clamped or bolted together later when molding work is being done (Fig. 5-27). The mold can then be taken apart for removing a molding and then put back together again for making the next one.

Another reason for making a mold in more than one piece is to avoid difficult lay-up jobs, such as deep areas that are hard to reach. To avoid this, the mold is made in two or more pieces, which are later bonded or mechanically fastened together.

If the mold is to be in more than one piece, this must be taken into account in the tooling and lay-up of the mold. Once the lay-up of the mold is completed, the resin is allowed to cure. Reinforcements, if required, are sometimes added before the plug is removed. In other cases, the plug is removed first, then the reinforcing members are added. These are attached to the mold by fiberglass bonding or other means.

Preparing the Mold for the Lay-up of the First Laminate. When the mold is completed, it is prepared for the lay-up or molding of the first laminate. It is generally easiest to do fiberglass lay-up work on a level or nearly level surface. Inclined and vertical surfaces are much more difficult. Overhead surfaces are nearly impossible and generally avoided.

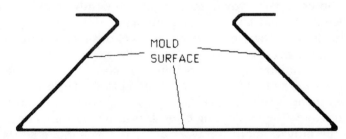

Fig. 5-26. Contact mold with undercuts.

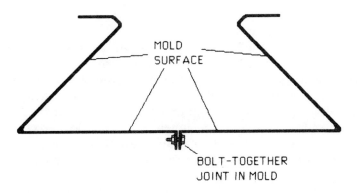

MOLD
SURFACE

BOLT-TOGETHER
JOINT IN MOLD

Fig. 5-27. Contact mold with undercuts made in two sections.

If there is no other way, special resins are available that make overhead lay-up work at least possible.

The mold is usually positioned so that most of the lay-up work is done from directly above. For a bathtub or similar mold, however, no single position of the mold will be satisfactory. This difficulty can either be put up with (the sides of the tub laid up on a vertical plane) or the mold can be arranged so that it can be turned various angles for different phases of the lay-up. The mold is then angled so that the area where the lay-up work is being done is as nearly level or horizontal as possible. This is usually a fairly simple matter in the case of a small mold, but it can be much more difficult in the case of large molds, such as for a swimming pool. Special hoists and other equipment are frequently used for changing the angle of the mold. Some molds are mounted on half-round wheels so that the mold can be easily rotated from side to side.

To get ready for a lay-up, the mold is first cleaned. Wax is then applied and buffed out. A parting agent such as PVA is then applied to the mold surface. After the first few moldings are made, the wax alone may be enough to allow removal of moldings from the mold.

Lay-up of Laminate Layers. The first layer of the laminate is usually a gel coat of the desired color. In manufacturing processes, this is sprayed on, but it can also be applied by brush if spray equipment and supporting protective and safety equipment are not available. A recent trend is to omit the gel coat on some moldings and then to paint the molding later after it has been taken from the mold. The reasons for this are problems with the gel coat (cracking, crazing, and color fading) and difficulty of application. Also, gel coats are frequently damaged when the molding is taken from the mold, which requires difficult touch-up work, and paints for use on fiberglass have improved greatly over the years. Using two-part polyurethane paint, it is possible to get a gel coat-like appearance that is in many ways more durable than traditional gel coat applications.

The gel coat, if used, will be the finished side of the laminate. If the gel coat is not used, a surface coat of resin is applied instead. The gel coat is allowed to harden. Because an air-inhibited resin is usually used, the surface on the exposed side will remain tacky.

The next layer of the laminate is usually fiberglass mat, although a lightweight cloth with a smooth finish is sometimes used. A thin layer of resin is applied over the gel coat. The mat is placed over the wet resin. Additional resin is applied to the mat until it is saturated with resin.

The remaining layers of the laminate are added over the first layer of mat. The laminate should be designed to give the desired characteristics to the molding for its particular application. The laminate may be all mat layers. Cloth and/or woven roving may be alternated with mat layers.

Considerable care in the lay-up work is needed to produce quality laminates. The proper ratio of resin to reinforcing material, which varies depending on the reinforcing material used, should be kept as close to the ideal ratio as possible. Resin-rich (too much resin) and resin-starved (too little resin) areas should be avoided.

Sometimes, instead of laying up the laminate by hand, a chopper gun is used. This is a spraying device that mixes catalyst and resin and chops up strands of fiberglass, and sprays the mixture onto the mold. This mixture is applied over the gel coat layer until the desired thickness of laminate is achieved—all in one operation. This method is much faster than the hand lay-up, but a generally poorer quality laminate results. Still, for many applications it is adequate. A highly skilled operator is needed to spray up a laminate of even thickness or to desired varying thicknesses without getting too much resin for the amount of chopped glass fiber reinforcing strands or, less frequently, too little resin.

Moldings can also be made by combinations of hand lay-up and spray-up with a chopper gun. For example, the chopper gun can be used to replace layers of mat, with fiberglass cloth and woven roving laid up by hand over wet layers of the spray-up. The cloth and woven roving are usually saturated with resin by brush or roller application. Allow for curing before adding the next spray-up layer.

Large Moldings. Large moldings present special problems. Many pieces of reinforcing material will have to be used. When joining pieces, they are usually overlapped from about 1 to 6 inches, depending on the particular application (Fig. 5-28). These overlaps must not all be made in the same areas if an even thickness is desired. The overlaps are made at random in most cases. In some moldings the cloth and woven roving reinforcing materials run continuously the length of the molding in one direction, or other specific patterns are used to give desired structural strength to the laminate.

The thickness of the laminate is often varied to give the greatest strength and/or stiffness in the areas where needed. This presents additional difficulties in the lay-up of the laminate. The idea is to put the materials where they will do the most good.

On a large laminate, even one additional layer of reinforcing mate-

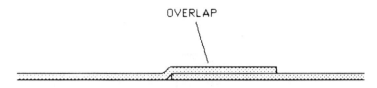

OVERLAP

Fig. 5-28. Reinforcing material is overlapped.

rial can add greatly to the material and labor cost of the lay-up. For this reason, manufacturers try to design laminates to be strong enough for the way they will be used, plus a safety margin, while still using the minimum of materials and labor cost.

Most large moldings require a number of days for the lay-up work to be completed. One layer of reinforcing is saturated with resin at a time and is allowed to harden before the next layer is added. This makes it easier to remove air bubbles and wrinkles in the lay-up. Sometimes two and even three layers are added on top of each other before any have set. This is not a job for an inexperienced fiberglasser to tackle, however.

Most lay-up work in manufacturing is done during 8-hour workdays, often with no lay-up work being done on weekends. This requires careful logistics to keep track of the lay-up work that has been done and what needs to be done next. There is usually a laminating schedule. Each job is checked off as soon as it is completed. A do-it-yourselfer might face similar problems in logistics.

Layers of laminates are occasionally left out of moldings. In some cases, this is accidental. In others it is done to reduce the cost. Sometimes unsafe products result. In one instance, a boat with a fiberglass hull split and sank. It was recovered and the damage analyzed. The hull, it turned out, had only about half the advertised thickness in the area of damage, and several layers of reinforcing material had been left out. There was a lawsuit over this incident.

Most large moldings require additional reinforcement in the form of beams (Fig. 5-29), stringers (Fig. 5-30), ribs (Fig. 5-31), hat sections (Fig. 5-32), and so on. This is a more efficient use of materials than attempting to achieve the same results by increasing the laminate's thickness. Adding reinforcements is covered in later chapters along with specific projects where they are required. Moldings that are taken from a mold might require additional attachments. In some cases separate moldings must be joined together.

When the lay-up of a molding has been completed, the laminate is allowed to cure for a certain length of time, usually from several hours to several days depending on the type and size of the laminate and other factors, before it is removed from the mold. Most manufacturers want to remove the molding from the mold as soon as possible so that another molding can be started. However, moldings can be damaged or ruined if they are taken from the mold too soon. The do-it-yourselfer can

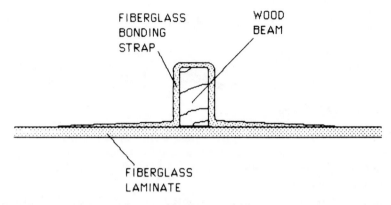

Fig. 5-29. Beam used to reinforce fiberglass laminate.

usually wait extra time to be sure that molding has cured properly.

Removing Moldings from Mold. Even though the molds are waxed and PVA is applied to the mold before the lay-up, it is often difficult to remove moldings, especially large ones, from the molds. You may have gotten some idea of this from the introductory practice projects with a very small mold. For large moldings, hoists are often used for "breaking" the molding from the mold.

Once the molding is removed from the mold, the wax and polyvinyl alcohol (PVA) are cleaned from the gel coat. Touch-up work is usually required on the gel coat, because it is difficult to achieve perfection in the original molding, especially if it is a large one. Some moldings will require more extensive repairs and some might even be rejected. Some moldings from the same mold turn out better than others.

Core Constructions with Double Skins and Other Contact Moldings. Contact moldings can be made not only with single skin laminates, as detailed above, but also with core constructions with double skins. Typical core materials include honeycomb cell paper, foamed plastics (Fig. 5-33), and wood, especially balsa (Fig. 5-34) and plywood (Fig. 5-35).

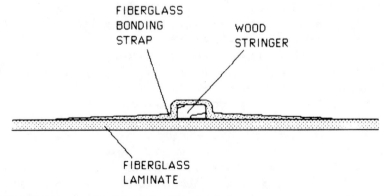

Fig. 5-30. Stringer used to reinforce fiberglass laminate.

84

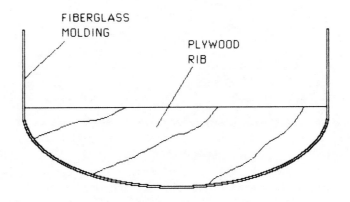

Fig. 5-31. Rib used to reinforce fiberglass laminate.

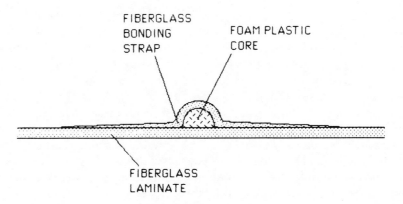

Fig. 5-32. Hat section used to reinforce fiberglass laminate.

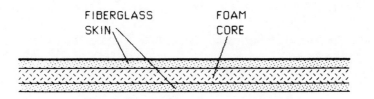

Fig. 5-33. Contact molded laminate with plastic core and double skins.

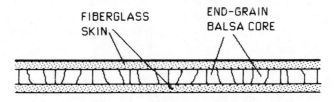

Fig. 5-34. Contact molded laminate with balsa core and double skins.

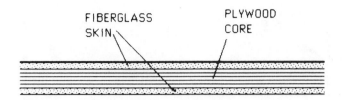

Fig. 5-35. Contact molded laminate with plywood core and double skins.

Regardless of the core material used, the first skin or laminate is usually laid up in the mold as described earlier. The core material is placed over a wet layer (saturated with resin) of reinforcing material or otherwise bonded to the laminate. A second skin is then laminated over the core material. This is usually all done before the laminate is removed from the mold.

In some cases various other structural reinforcements are also added to the laminate before it is removed from the mold. The structure of the laminate must be such that it will retain its shape when removed from the mold. Care must also be taken to properly support the molding if it is taken from the mold before fully cured, or before structural reinforcing has been added.

Sometimes the molding is the finished product when it comes out of the mold. Bathtubs and hot tubs are typical examples. Other times moldings will require additional construction and assembly. Some moldings are only a small part of the total construction. For example, a travel trailer may have only the roof made of fiberglass, with the rest of the construction of wood, metal, and other materials.

Some moldings are laidup upside down, such as tubs; others are molded right side up, such as a boat hull. Special equipment is required for turning over large moldings. This is sometimes done with the item still in the mold. In other cases it is removed from the mold upside down and then turned over.

Quality of Contact Moldings. It is important to be able to recognize contact moldings and have some idea of the quality of the laminates. You will also need to judge the quality of laminates that you make. Fiberglass moldings that are formed by contact molding can usually be recognized because the backside is not as smooth and even as the side that was against the mold, which is usually gel coated or painted.

Often it will be possible to tell if the contact molding was hand-laid-up or sprayed up with a chopper gun. Examine the back side of the molding. Overlapping of reinforcing material and/or the weave of cloth or woven roving indicates hand lay-up, or at least a combination of spray-up and hand lay-up. A spray-up laminate will show chopped strands of fiberglass with a matlike appearance, except there will be no overlapping of pieces of mat reinforcing material.

Woven roving on the back side of the laminate indicates not only hand lay-up, but also that heavy reinforcing materials were used. This can be important in situations where a strong laminate is required.

Other clues to the quality of manufactured contact moldings include:

● Thickness: How does the thickness of the product compare to those made by other manufacturers? While a thicker laminate does not necessarily mean a stronger one, it often does.

● Fairness: If possible, sight along the finished side of the molding. It should be smooth and even. Lack of fairness indicates that a poor mold was used and/or that the molding was not properly reinforced.

● Ability to support loads: When you put weight on the laminate, how much does it give? The amount acceptable depends on how the laminate is to be used. The laminate should be able to support all loads normally placed on it without undue flexing.

● The gel coat: The gel coat often gives a good indication of the quality of the entire laminate. Cracking, crazing, and fading of gel coat indicate poor quality of materials and/or poor application of the gel coating. This often indicates lack of quality in the remainder of the laminate. A good gel coat, in turn, indicates the use of quality materials and proper application of them. This is especially true if the laminate has been in use for a long time.

PRESSURE MOLDING

In an attempt to get around some of the problems associated with contact molding, various methods of pressure molding, including matched die or double mold technique, pressure bag, and vacuum bag, are sometimes used. Of these techniques, only the matched die or double mold technique has much application for do-it-yourselfers. The other methods require expensive specialized equipment.

Introductory Pressure Molding Project

One of the simplest pressure molding techniques is the matched die or double mold. The flat mold used for the introductory contact molding project is used again for this introductory project. For the double mold technique, you will need to construct a matching flat mold. This will allow for making a flat laminate that has a smooth finished surface on both sides. The introductory project is to mold a 10- x -10-inch flat square of fiberglass that can be used as a decorative pad on a tabletop or for other similar uses. Unlike the pad molded in the introductory contact molding project, the double molded pad will have a smooth finished surface on both sides. The only required sanding and finishing work that will be required is on the edges.

Making the Mold. The first step is to make matching half of the mold, which is a 10-by-10-inch square of 1/2-inch plywood. the decorative pad could, of course, be a larger or smaller size by changing the mold size, but the 10- x -10-inch size is ideal for a first project. Mark and cut the plywood (Fig. 5-36).

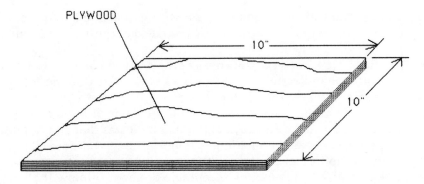

PLYWOOD

10"

10"

Fig. 5-36. Plywood for upper half of flat pressure mold.

Because the surface of the plywood will be used to mold the upper surface of the molding, it must be smooth and prepared so that the molding will not stick.

While various methods can be used to make the wood surface suitable, most frequently a thin layer of polyester resin is applied to the surface, allowed to cure, and then the surface is sanded and buffed until it is very smooth.

In addition to the 1/2-inch thick plywood cut previously to a 10-inch square, you will need either finishing or general purpose polyester resin (gel coat resin is not used here), and the rest of the items on the materials list.

Place the plywood on the protective paper with the mold surface upward. Carefully stir the resin with a clean stirring stick. Pour 1 ounce of resin into the mixing cup. Replace the lid on the resin container and set it aside.

If available, add about 1/8 ounce of styrene monomer to the resin and mix thoroughly. The resin can be applied to the plywood surface without this, but the thinning action of the styrene allows it to better penetrate the surface of the wood.

Add 8 drops of catalyst to the ounce of resin. This is approximately 2 percent by volume, which should give about 15 minutes of working time. Wait about 30 seconds, then brush a smooth thin layer of the catalyzed resin onto the mold surface of the plywood (Fig. 5-2). When you have finished applying the resin, clean the paint brush with acetone before the resin hardens. Allow the resin to harden on the plywood surface for at least an hour before attempting to sand it.

Lightly sand the surface with fine-grit paper to remove the surfacing agent. This is not necessary if laminating resin is used. You can also remove the surfacing agent by wiping the surface with acetone on a rag. Apply a second coat of polyester resin, and when this has cured, apply a third coat. When the third coat has cured, sand with fine grit wet/dry sandpaper and water using a sanding block.

Polish the surface using a buffing compound. This can be done by hand with a clean cloth, or use a power buffer.

Take time to make a good mold. Any defects in the mold surface will be copied on the moldings made with the mold.

This completes the construction of the upper section of the flat mold for the introductory pressure molding project.

Molding the Pad. To mold the pad, you will need the two matching flat molds, a large cement building block or other suitable weight for applying downward pressure on the upper section of the mold, a 1 1/2-ounce fiberglass mat 12 × 12 inches square, and the items on the materials list.

Now you can follow the basic instructions given earlier in this chapter, Steps 1 through 13.

In Step 2, refer to Fig. 5-3.

In Step 3, use 4 ounces of the gel coat resin.

In Step 4, use 32 drops of catalyst.

In Step 5, laminate a layer of fiberglass mat reinforcing material to the bottom mold surface over the gel coat (Fig. 5-4). Because 1 square foot of 1 1/2-ounce mat weighs approximately 1 1/2 ounces, the amount of resin required to saturate or wet out the reinforcing material can be calculated. Mat laminates are typically 25 to 35 percent fiberglass reinforcing material and 65 to 75 percent resin by weight. For a 25 percent mat ratio, about triple the weight of the mat in resin is required to fully wet out the mat. One and one-half ounces multiplied by three is 4 1/2 ounces. To allow for some waste and to be certain you will have enough resin, 5 ounces can be used.

In Step 6, if you use 12 drops of catalyst for 1 ounce of resin, here you will use 60 drops for 5 ounces.

In Step 9, refer to Fig. 5-37.

Complete Step 9, but don't clean the brush. Before the laminate has had a chance to set up, turn the upper half of the mold so that the cured gel coat surface is face down and press it in place on top of the wet layer of mat. Apply pressure downward and rock the mold back and forth to work out any air. Then place the cement building block or other suitable weight on top of the upper half of the mold. Make sure that the upper half of the mold is level so that the laminate will have an equal thickness. When everything looks okay, clean the resin from the brush with acetone.

Go on to Step 13 from here.

At this stage of the introductory project, you have moved from chemical construction to working with cured fiberglass.

Finishing the Introductory Double-mold Project. The next step is to mark the pattern for the 10-inch square and saw off excess laminate (about an inch all the way around). Sawing methods are detailed above in this chapter.

File and sand the edges smooth. Round the edges slightly, as shown in Fig. 5-38.

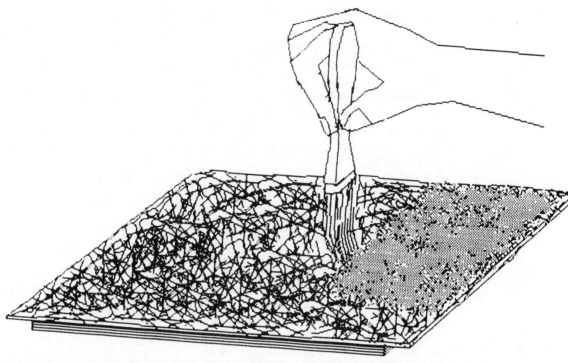

Fig. 5-37. The fiberglass mat on the lower section of the mold is saturated with polyester resin.

Polish and buff the gel coat surfaces and edges of the laminate. This completes the introductory flat pressure molding project.

Other Laminates Using the Same Pressure Mold

The same flat two-section pressure mold can be used for a variety of laminates. By making these laminates, you can learn the fundamentals of pressure molding on a simple flat mold before going on to more complicated molds.

Single Layer Cloth Laminate. To pressure mold a single layer cloth laminate (Fig. 5-39), you will need the same two-part mold as used for the introductory pressure molding project detailed above, a piece of 10-ounce fiberglass cloth 12 × 12 inches square, and the items on the materials list.

Now follow the basic instructions, beginning with Step 1.

In Step 3, use 2 ounces of the gel coat resin.

In Step 4, add 16 drops of catalyst.

In Step 5, because 1 square yard of 10 ounce cloth weighs approximately 10 ounces, the approximate amount of resin required to saturate or wet out the reinforcing material can be calculated. Cloth laminates are typically 45 to 50 percent fiberglass cloth reinforcing material and 50 to 55 percent resin by weight. For a 50 percent cloth ratio, the weight of the resin should be equal to the weight of the cloth. A 12-inch square

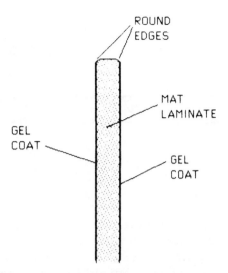

Fig. 5-38. Round edges of laminate slightly with file.

is 1/9 of a square yard, which weighs slightly less than 1 ounce. Thus, you will need approximately 1 ounce of resin to saturate the cloth.

In Step 6, then, you use 12 drops of catalyst for 1 ounce of resin.

After Step 9, before the laminate has had a chance to set up, turn the upper half of the mold so that the cured gel coat surface is face down and press it in place on top of the wet layer of cloth. Apply pressure downward and rock the mold back and forth to work out any air. Then place the cement building block or other suitable weight on top of the upper half of the mold. Make sure that the upper half of the mold is level so that the laminate will have an equal thickness.

Clean the resin from the brush and go on to Steps 12 through 15.

Single-layer Woven Roving Laminate. To pressure mold a single-layer woven roving laminate (Fig. 5-40), you will need the same two-part mold used for the introductory pressure molding project, a cement building block or other suitable weight to apply pressure to the mold, a piece of 24-ounce fiberglass woven roving 12 × 12 inches square, and the items on the materials list.

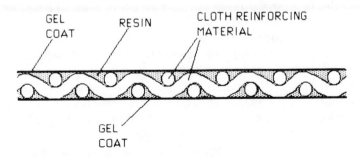

Fig. 5-39. Pressure molded single-layer cloth laminate.

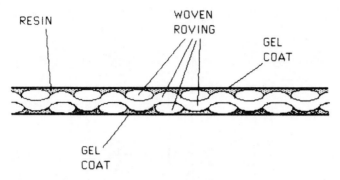

RESIN

WOVEN
ROVING

GEL
COAT

GEL
COAT

Fig. 5-40. Pressure molded single-layer woven roving laminate.

Now follow the basic instructions, starting with Step 1.

In Step 3, use 2 ounces of the gel coat resin.

In Step 4, add 16 drops of catalyst to the ounce of resin.

In Step 5, because 1 square yard of 24-ounce woven roving weighs approximately 24 ounces, the amount of resin required to saturate or wet out the reinforcing material can be calculated. Woven roving laminates are typically 40 to 45 percent fiberglass woven roving reinforcing material and 55 to 60 percent resin by weight. The weight of the resin will be slightly more than the weight of the woven roving. A 12-inch square is 1/9 of a square yard, which weighs approximately 2.7 ounces (calculated as 24 divided by 9). Thus, you will need 3 ounces of resin to saturate the woven roving.

In Step 6, use 3 ounces of resin. Use 12 drops of catalyst for 1 ounce of resin, or 36 drops for the 3 ounces of resin. So in Step 7, add the 36 drops of catalyst.

After Step 9, proceed as you did for the cloth laminate: before the laminate has had a chance to set up, turn the upper half of the mold so that the cured gel coat surface is face down and press it in place on top of the wet layer of cloth. Apply pressure downward and rock the mold back and forth to work out any air. Then place the cement building block or other suitable weight on top of the upper half of the mold. Make sure that the upper half of the mold is level so that the laminate will have an equal thickness.

Clean the resin from the brush and go on to Steps 12 through 15.

Two-layer Mat Laminate. Two layers of the same reinforcing material can be pressure molded together. To mold a two-layer mat laminate (Fig. 5-41), you will need the same two-part mold used for the introductory pressure molding project, a cement building block or other suitable weight to apply pressure to the mold, two pieces of 1 1/2-ounce fiberglass mat 12 x 12 inches square, plus the items on the materials list.

Now follow the basic instructions, starting with Step 1.

In Step 3, use 2 ounces of gel coat resin.

In Step 4, add 16 drops of catalyst to the ounce of resin.

Pressure molding generally works best if the resin is applied to all layers of reinforcing material before any of them have been allowed to set up.

In Step 5, because 1 square foot of 1 1/2-ounce mat weighs approximately 1 1/2 ounces, the approximate amount of resin required to saturate or wet out the two layers of reinforcing material can be calculated. Mat laminates are typically 25 to 35 percent fiberglass reinforcing material and 65 to 75 percent resin by weight. For a 25 percent mat ratio, about triple the weight of the mat in resin is required to fully wet out the mat. Three times 1 1/2 ounces times two is 9 ounces. To allow for waste use 10 ounces.

In Step 6, use 10 ounces of resin. If you use 12 drops of catalyst for 1 ounce of resin, you use 120 for 10 ounces. So in Step 7, add 120 drops of catalyst.

After Step 9, don't clean the brush. Position the second fiberglass mat layer over the wet resin of the first layer so it is centered, and press it down and smooth it out. Saturate the mat with resin, using the brush with a dabbing action.

Before the laminate has had a chance to set up, turn the upper half of the mold so that the cured gel coat surface is face down and press it in place on top of the wet layer of mat. Apply pressure downward and rock the mold back and forth to work out any air. Then place the cement building block or other suitable weight on top of the upper half of the mold. Make sure that the upper half of the mold is level so that the laminate will have an equal thickness. Clean the resin from the brush with acetone.

Now go on to Steps 12 through 15.

Two-layer Cloth Laminate. To mold a two-layer cloth laminate by pressure molding (Fig. 5-42), you will need the same two-part mold used for the introductory pressure molding project, a cement building block or other suitable weight to apply pressure to the mold, two pieces of 10-ounce fiberglass cloth 12 × 12 inches square, and the items on the materials list.

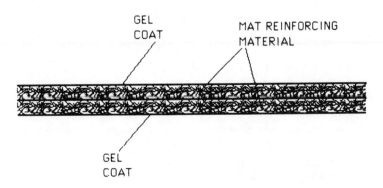

GEL COAT

MAT REINFORCING MATERIAL

GEL COAT

Fig. 5-41. Pressure molded two-layer mat laminate.

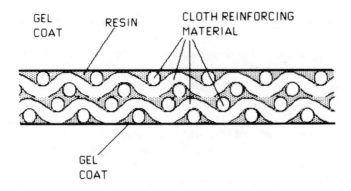

GEL COAT   RESIN   CLOTH REINFORCING MATERIAL

GEL COAT

Fig. 5-42. Pressure molded two-layer cloth laminate.

Now follow the basic instructions, beginning with Step 1.

In Step 3, use 2 ounces of the gel coat resin.

In Step 4, Add 16 drops of catalyst to the resin.

In Step 5, because 1 square yard of 10-ounce cloth weighs approximately 10 ounces, the approximate amount of resin required to saturate or wet out the reinforcing material can be calculated. Cloth laminates are typically 45 to 50 percent fiberglass cloth reinforcing material and 50 to 55 percent resin by weight. For a 50 percent cloth ratio, the weight of the resin should be equal to the weight of the cloth. A 12-inch square is 1/9 of a square yard, which weighs slightly less than 1 ounce. Thus, you will need approximately 1 ounce of resin to saturate each layer of the cloth, or 2 ounces for both layers.

In Step 6, use 2 ounces of resin. Use 24 drops of catalyst for 2 ounces of resin. So in Step 7, add 120 drops of catalyst.

After Step 9, don't clean the brush. Position the second layer of fiberglass cloth over the wet resin of the first layer so it is centered, and press it down and smooth it out. Saturate the cloth with resin.

Before the laminate has had a chance to set up, turn the upper half of the mold so that the cured gel coat surface is face down and press it in place on top of the wet layer of cloth. Apply pressure downward and rock the mold back and forth to work out any air. Then place the cement building block or other suitable weight on top of the upper half of the mold. Make sure that the upper half of the mold is level so that the laminate will have an equal thickness. Clean the resin from the brush with acetone before the resin hardens.

Now go on to Steps 12 through 15.

Two-layer Woven Roving Laminate. To pressure mold a two-layer woven roving laminate (Fig. 5-43), you will need the same two-part mold used for the introductory pressure molding project, a cement building block or other suitable weight to apply pressure to the mold, two pieces of 24-ounce fiberglass woven roving 12 × 12 inches square, plus the items on the materials list.

In Step 3, use 2 ounces of the gel coat resin.

In Step 4, add 16 drops of catalyst to the resin.

In Step 5, because 1 square yard of 24-ounce woven roving weighs approximately 24 ounces, the amount of resin required to saturate or wet out the reinforcing material can be calculated. Woven roving laminates are typically 40 to 45 percent fiberglass woven roving reinforcing material and 55 to 60 percent resin by weight. Thus, the weight of the resin will be slightly more than the weight of the woven roving. A 12-inch square is 1/9 of a square yard, which weighs approximately 2.7 ounces (calculated as 24 divided by 9). Thus, you will need approximately 3 ounces of resin to saturate one of the pieces of woven roving, or 6 ounces for both of them.

In Step 6, use 6 ounces of resin. For 6 ounces of resin, use 72 drops of catalyst.

After Step 9, don't clean the brush. Position the second layer of fiberglass woven roving over the wet resin of the first layer, press it down, and smooth it out. The brush can be used for this. Remember that, unlike with mat, a brushing action can be used, but be careful not to unravel the cut edges of the woven roving. Saturate the woven roving with resin.

Before the laminate has had a chance to set up, turn the upper half of the mold so that the cured gel coat surface is face down and press it in place on top of the wet layer of cloth. Apply pressure downward and rock the mold back and forth to work out any air. Then place the cement building block or other suitable weight on top of the upper half of the mold. Make sure that the upper half of the mold is level so that the laminate will have an equal thickness. Clean the brush.

Now go on to Steps 12 through 15.

This completes the two-layer woven roving laminate pressure molding project.

Pressure Molding with More Than Two Layers of the Same Kind of Reinforcing Material. Using the same two-part mold and technique, it is possible to mold three or more layers of the same reinforcing material, although this becomes more difficult as more layers are attempted.

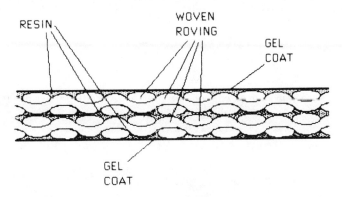

Fig. 5-43. Pressure molded two-layer woven roving laminate.

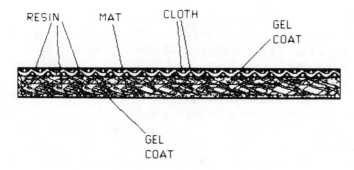

Fig. 5-44. Pressure molded two-layer mat and cloth laminate.

Pressure Molding with More Than One Kind of Reinforcing Material.
In a similar manner laminates can be laid up with more than one kind
of reinforcing material. Mat and cloth are frequently used to form two-
layer (Fig. 5-44) and three-layer (Fig. 5-45) moldings. Mat is also frequently used with woven roving to fill in the coarse weave pattern of
the woven roving and give a better bond between layers (Fig. 5-46). In
some cases, mat, cloth, and woven roving is used in the same laminate
(Fig. 5-47).

Pressure Molding Methods

The above flat pressure molding projects serve as an introduction to pressure molding.

Matched Die Molding. The introductory projects using a double flat
mold are examples of matched die molding. This is a pressure method
of molding a fiberglass laminate by squeezing catalyzed resin and fiberglass reinforcing materials between two molds (Fig. 5-48).

This method works well for certain types of fiberglass molding. It
gives a quality laminate that is smooth and formed on both sides. As
a manufacturing method, a proper ratio of resin to glass fiber reinforcement can be maintained with modern molding equipment. Production
is much more rapid than when contact molding is used, especially when
the molds are heated to speed up the curing time.

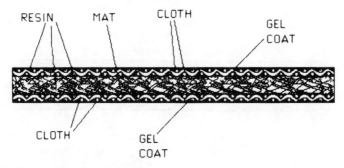

Fig. 5-45. Pressure molded three-layer mat and cloth laminate.

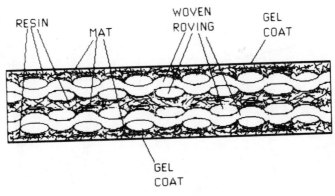

Fig. 5-46. Pressure molded mat and woven roving laminate.

Disadvantages: It is expensive to tool for matched die molding and that this method is generally limited to fairly small moldings. Applying gel coat in a matched die mold can be difficult. Matched die moldings are frequently painted instead. It is also possible to add a color pigment to all the resin used. The color resin will then be throughout the laminate. However, this method has only limited usefulness, because the glass fibers will usually show through the surface.

Manufacturers generally use matched die molding only when large numbers of the same molding are required. The tooling is very expensive and must be amortized by making many moldings.

Simple matched die molds can be constructed however, such as were used for the introductory projects. Mat and/or other reinforcing materials can be applied to one surface of the mold by hand. The matched die mold can then be set in place and clamped down in the desired position. Most production equipment does some or all of these jobs automatically.

Modern matched die molding used in manufacturing allows rapid molding cycles. For example, a fiberglass sports car top having an area of about 20 square feet has a molding cycle of about five minutes in matched die molding, whereas it commonly takes several hours or more using hand lay-up in a contact mold. Before switching to matched die

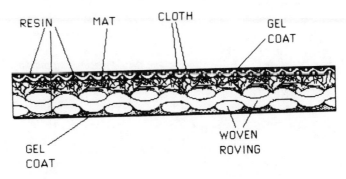

Fig. 5-47. Pressure molded cloth, mat, and woven roving laminate.

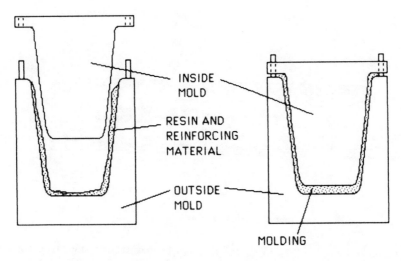

INSIDE
MOLD

RESIN AND
REINFORCING
MATERIAL

OUTSIDE
MOLD

MOLDING

Fig. 5-48. Matched die fiberglass molding.

molding, many manufacturers first use molding methods that have less tooling cost to make certain that there is enough demand for the product to justify the high tooling cost required for matched die molding.

From a do-it-yourselfer point of view, matched die or double mold techniques are ideal for certain types of construction projects, as detailed in later chapters.

Pressure Bag Molding. Pressure bag molding uses one rigid die, with the opposite die made of a flexible rubber-like material (Fig. 5-49). The required amount of catalyzed resin and reinforcing material is fed into the mold. Air pressure is forced into the area above the bag. This squeezes the resin and reinforcing material into the desired position, with a uniform surface against the bag. The pressure is maintained until the molded part has cured.

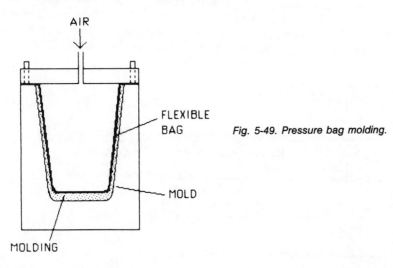

AIR

FLEXIBLE
BAG

Fig. 5-49. Pressure bag molding.

MOLD

MOLDING

98

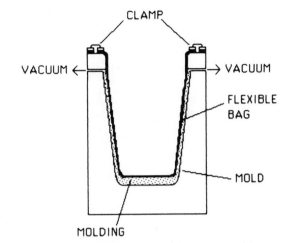

Fig. 5-50. Vacuum bag molding.

To speed the curing time, hot air or steam pressure can be used or the mold can be heated in some other manner. Using this method for manufacturing with modern equipment, items such as helmets can be molded in three-minute cycles.

Vacuum Bag Molding. Vacuum bag molding is similar to the pressure bag method, except that a vacuum is used between the rigid die and the bag (Fig. 5-50). The area between the bag and the rigid mold must be airtight for this method to work. Molding is done by first adding the required amount of reinforcing material and catalyzed resin to the mold. This is done automatically on modern systems. Vacuum is then applied, which draws the flexible bag down into the desired position, and squeezes the resin and reinforcing material into shape. This produces a uniform surface against the rigid die and a nearly uniform surface against the bag. The vacuum is maintained until the molded part has cured. Various means of applying external heat to the mold are used to speed the cure. Here, too, items such as helmets can be molded in three-minute cycles.

Chapter 6

Guideline for Projects

The instructions in Chapters 7 through 12 use the same basic materials. Refer to the following materials list as you progress.

MATERIALS LIST

1. Mold you are working with.
2. Laminating, finishing, or general-purpose polyester resin.
3. A paste-type mold release (which is used during the actual molding process, and therefore with steps 12 through 32).
4. Polyester gel coat resin (also used during the molding process and with steps 12 through 32).
5. Catalyst for the resin.
6. A mixing cup (the kind sold at drug stores with ounce markings on the side).
7. Small mixing sticks.
8. Longer mixing sticks.
9. A small paint brush for applying the resin.
10. Fiberglass reinforcing material (type, weight, and number depends on desired laminate, which varies with the projects).
11. Squeegies and laminating rollers (for larger projects).
12. Paper to protect the working area.
13. Proper protective clothing.
14. Decorative cloth or other materials to add to the fiberglass laminate (for some projects).

BASIC INSTRUCTIONS

The following basic instructions—with slight variations, which are noted—are used throughout Chapters 7 through 12.

In the chapters that follow, various molds are covered. In each instance, the mold can be formed from a variety of materials. Be sure to note whether contact or pressure molding is being used. When one smooth surface is required, you will be contact molding, when a molded surface is required on both sides, you will be pressure molding.

Because contact molding gives a smooth surface on one side only, there are two basic forms the molds can take. For example, if you want to mold a box with a smooth inside surface, the contact mold surface will look like the outside of an upside down box. Conversely, if you want this box to have a smooth outside surface, the contact surface will look like the inside of a box with an open top. Keep in mind that the molding is not a duplicate of the mold, but a reverse image.

Forming the Mold

Step 1. Ordinary woodworking techniques can be used to form the mold, and fine-grain wood is preferred. Molds can be shaped from a single piece of wood, or two or more pieces can be glued together.

Step 2. After the wood has been shaped and sanded, prepare the wood surface so that it is suitable for molding. One method is to coat the molding surface with a thin layer of polyester resin. In addition to the shaped and sanded wood mold, you will need either finishing or general purpose polyester resin, catalyst for the resin, a mixing cup (the kind sold at drug stores with ounce markings on the sides), a small mixing stick, one longer mixing stick that can be used to stir the resin in the container in which it was purchased, and a small paint brush for applying the resin. You will also need a piece of paper to protect the area where you will be working, which can be on a bench, floor, or concrete surface outside. Don't forget to follow safety rules and use proper equipment.

Step 3. Place the wood mold (or wood mold parts, or mock-up) with the molding surface upward. When you have everything ready, begin by opening the container that the resin came in. Carefully stir it with a clean stirring stick. When removing the stick from the container, allow as much of the resin to drain off the stick back into the container as possible. Use a clean rag to clean the remaining resin from the stick. Put the stick aside for later use. Keep this one stick for use only for stirring uncatalyzed resin in the containers in which it is sold.

Step 4. You will need about 1 ounce of resin for each square foot of wood surface to be covered. Pour the required amount of resin into the mixing cup. Use the markings on the sides of the cup as a guide, or you can use a measuring scoop such as the kind used in the kitchen (but don't use it for kitchen duty again after you have used it for measuring resin). Replace the lid on the resin container and set it aside.

Step 5. If available, add about 1/8 ounce of styrene monomer to the resin and mix thoroughly. While the resin can be applied to the wood surface without this, the thinning action of the styrene will serve to thin the resin and allow it to better penetrate the surface of the wood.

Step 6. Add 8 drops of catalyst for each ounce of resin to the resin. This is approximately 2 percent by volume, which should give about 15 minutes of working time. Wait about 30 seconds, then brush a smooth thin layer of the catalyzed resin onto the molding surface. When you have finished applying the coat of resin to the molding surface of the wood and everything looks alright, clean the paint brush with acetone. This must be done before the resin hardens if the brush is to be used again. Allow the resin to harden on the wood surface. Even though this should happen about 15 minutes after the resin is applied, it is best to wait at least an hour before attempting to sand the surface.

Step 7. Lightly sand the surface with fine-grit paper to remove the surfacing agent. This is not necessary if laminating resin is used. An alternate method is to remove the surfacing agent by wiping the surface with acetone.

Step 8. Apply a second coat of polyester resin in the same manner as detailed above. When this has cured, apply a third coat.

Step 9. When the third coat has cured, sand with fine-grit wet/dry sandpaper and water.

Step 10. Polish the surface using a buffing compound. This can be done by hand with a clean cloth, or use a power buffer.

Step 11. It is important to take the necessary time to make a good mold. Any defects in the mold surface will be copied on the moldings made with the mold.

A variety of forms can be used as molds. Trays, bowls or pans made of stainless steel and aluminum are ideal. Many plastic trays, bowls or pans will also work, but make certain that the plastic is a type that polyester resin will not dissolve. Keep in mind that you will not be making a duplicate of the tray or pan, but using it as a mold to obtain a reverse image.

When contact molding, you use one side of the tray or pan when laying up a molding, although many trays and pans will allow molding on either side. Make certain that the mold form does not have vertical sides or overhangs that will make removing a finished molding difficult or impossible.

When pressure molding, you will be concerned with both concave and convex molding forms: The main problem is to find mold halves that match.

While the mold can be placed directly over protective paper on a floor, it often is more convenient to work with the mold placed on a table or other suitable platform.

Molding

The following steps describe the actual process of molding:

Step 12. You will need a suitable mold, as detailed above, and the rest of the items on the materials list.

Step 13. Place the mold or molds on the protective paper with the mold surface upward. If the molding surface of the mold is concave, you will do the lay-up inside a pan form. If the molding surface of the mold is convex, you will do the lay-up over a cap-like form. In either case, apply a coat of the paste-type mold release, using a clean cloth to spread a thin layer of the release over the entire mold surface. The purpose of this is to keep the molding from sticking so that it can be removed after it has cured.

Step 14. Apply the gel coat on the mold surfaces over the mold release. When you have everything ready, carefully stir the resin. This can be clear resin or any desired color, or color pigments formulated for polyester gel coat resin can be added. Don't forget to allow as much of the resin to drain off the stick back into the container as possible when removing it, and to use a clean rag to clean off the remaining resin from the stick.

Step 15. Pour required amount (this depends on area to be covered; usually about 1 ounce per square foot is required) of the gel coat resin into a mixing cup.

Step 16. Add the catalyst to the resin. In the examples in this book, this will be approximately 2 percent by volume, which is usually used for polyester gel coat resin at 75 degrees Fahrenheit. However, this can vary for the particular brand of gel coat resin being used. Follow the manufacturer's directions. Wait about 30 seconds, then brush a smooth thin layer of the catalyzed gel coat resin onto the mold surface over the mold release agent. Use a continuous motion with the brush rather than painting back and forth. The gel coat should have a thickness of only .02 to .03 inch. A thicker layer will be brittle and subject to cracking and crazing. When you have finished, clean the paint brush.

Gel coat resin usually doesn't contain a wax additive, so the laminate can be laid up directly over this with no additional surface preparation.

Step 17. Laminate the first layer of fiberglass reinforcing material (which is usually mat) to the gel coat. The reinforcing material should be cut to a size slightly larger than is required to cover the molding area of the mold (or in cases of duplication, the object to be duplicated). When working with deep rectangular forms and compound curves, cuts with lap joints are usually required to form the dry mat to the approximate shape. When pressure molding, keep in mind that in some cases only one layer of reinforcing material will be required. Other projects require two or more layers. If the double mold method is employed, it works best if all layers are laid up wet and at the same time.

Beginners are advised to apply one layer of reinforcing material at a time and allow this to set before applying the next layer. As experience is gained, two or more layers (up to a maximum of about 6 ounces of reinforcing material per square foot) can be applied wet. This is more difficult than applying a single layer at a time—and should therefore be tackled by more experienced fiberglassers—but makes the work faster.

Step 18. Mat can usually be formed to shallow curves without making cuts, but only after the resin has been applied to the material. Sharp curves and angles usually require making cuts and overlapping the mat in these areas. The overlaps can be worked down to an even thickness— after resin has been applied—by using a dabbing action of a paintbrush.

Step 19. Calculate the amount of resin required for saturating the reinforcing material that is to be applied wet at this time. Methods for determining the amount of resin required for various weights of reinforcing material were given in Chapter 5.

Step 20. Pour the required amount of resin into a mixing cup. You will probably need about 7 1/2 minutes of working time to apply the resin to a single layer of reinforcing material; more time might be required for multiple layers. Methods for determining the amount of catalyst to add to give desired working times at various temperatures were given in Chapter 5.

Step 21. Add the required amount of catalyst to the resin and stir. Wait about 30 seconds. Then, using the paint brush, apply a coat of resin over the gel coat layer that was applied to the mold surface and allowed to set previously.

Step 22. Position the first layer of fiberglass reinforcing material (usually a mat layer) over the wet resin so it is centered and press it down and smooth it out. For mat, use a dabbing action rather than a brushing action to avoid lumping up the mat.

Step 23. Saturate the reinforcing material with resin. Spread the resin as evenly as possible. Saturate all areas evenly, including areas of the reinforcing material that extend slightly beyond the desired size of the finished form (these will be trimmed off later after the laminate has cured).

Step 24. Note: This step applies to *contact* molding. For larger forms (which should not be attempted until considerable experience has been gained making small moldings), a squeegee or laminating roller can be used to remove air bubbles. The panels required for the projects detailed later in this chapter can be made without joints in the individual layers of reinforcing material by purchasing the reinforcing material in large enough sizes. However, if joints are required, the basic technique is to overlap the pieces about 1 to 2 inches. If mat is used, the laminate can be worked down to a nearly even thickness with a dabbing action of the brush when applying resin to the overlap.

Step 25. If a second layer of reinforcing material is to be applied wet over the first layer, position it in the wet resin and press it down and smooth it out. The brush can be used for this. If the second layer is cloth or woven roving rather than mat, a brushing action can be used, but be careful not to unravel the cut edges of the cloth.

Step 26. Saturate the second layer of reinforcing material with resin. Spread the resin as evenly as possible. All areas of the reinforcing material should be saturated.

Step 27. Apply all layers of reinforcing material that are to be applied wet at this time. When pressure molding, before the laminate has a chance to set up, turn the upper half of the mold so that the cured gel coat surface is face down, and press it in place on top of the wet layer of fiberglass reinforcing material. When everything looks alright, clean the resin from the brush with acetone. This must be done before the resin hardens if the brush is to be used again.

Step 28. It generally works best if laminating resin is used for all but the final layer of resin on the backside of the laminate. This final layer should be sanding or finishing resin to give a surface that is not sticky, so that it can be sanded.

Step 29. Allow the laminate to cure. If additional layer or layers of reinforcing material are to be added to the laminate, measure out and catalyze the required amount of polyester resin. Brush on a layer of wet resin over the cured laminate. Position the first resin so it is centered and press it down and smooth it out. The brush can be used for this.

Step 30. Saturate the reinforcing material with resin, spreading as evenly as possible. If additional layers are to be applied wet, these should be added at this time in a similar manner.

Step 31. Allow the laminate to thoroughly cure. Then remove it from the mold (or in the case of duplication, the object being duplicated). Even though the mold release was used, it still might be necessary to pry the laminate loose with a putty knife or other similar tool.

This completes the chemical part of the construction. For most projects, the fiberglass molding requires trimming. First mark pattern and saw off excess fiberglass at lip of tray or pan form. Sawing methods are detailed in Chapter 5.

Step 32. File and sand the edges smooth. Polish and buff the gel coat surfaces and edges of the laminate. (This step might not be necessary for some projects).

Chapter 7

Projects for Single
or Double Flat Molds

For projects using single or double flat molds, the basic idea is to form
flat panels of fiberglass that can be used for room screens, as panels
for cabinet doors, or formed into place mats, lamp shades, trays,
tabletops, and many other items.

All of the projects detailed in this chapter require molding flat panels
of fiberglass. To make these projects, refer to general instructions in
Chapter 6. For flat molds, you will begin with Step 13. Refer to the illustrations for this chapter as you progress.

FORMING PANELS BY CONTACT MOLDING

Basic methods for contact molding were introduced in Chapter 5.

Single Flat Molds

Plywood is frequently used for making the mold surface of single flat
molds. The first step is to cut the plywood to the desired size. Generally, this is slightly larger than the desired panel size. If a variety of sizes
are to be molded, the plywood should be larger than the largest desired
size.

For the introductory projects given in Chapter 5, the plywood surface is prepared by applying a thin coat of polyester resin and then sanding and polishing this to a smooth surface. Lacquer can be used in a
similar manner.

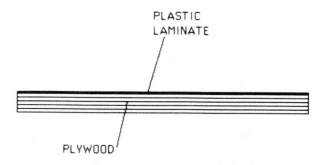

PLASTIC
LAMINATE

PLYWOOD

Fig. 7-1. Plastic laminate cemented to plywood for use as flat mold.

A generally better method, I have found, is to cement a plastic laminate to the plywood (Fig. 7-1). This can be attached with contact cement of the kind formulated for attaching plastic laminates to wood. Apply a thin layer to both the plywood surface and the bonding side of the plastic laminate. Allow the cement to dry. Position a piece of construction paper over the dry contact cement on the plywood. Then position the plastic laminate cement-side down on the paper. When you have the plastic laminate property lined up, slide the paper out. Use a block of wood and a hammer to lightly tap the laminate in place.

Wax and mold release can then be applied to the plastic laminate to prepare it for molding.

While the mold can be placed directly over protective paper on a floor, it often is more convenient to work with the mold placed on a table or other suitable platform.

Molding Flat Panels. To mold a flat panel, you will need a flat mold,

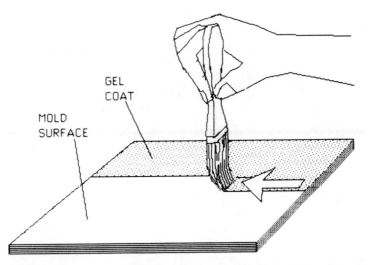

GEL
COAT

MOLD
SURFACE

Fig. 7-2. A thin layer of catalyzed polyester gel coat resin is brushed onto the mold surface over release agent.

as detailed in the preceding section. You will also need the items on the materials list in Chapter 6.

Now follow the basic instructions given in Chapter 6. Begin with Step 13, and work through to Step 32. (Disregard Step 18.) Refer to Figs. 7-2 through 7-9.

Double Flat Molds

The bottom half of the mold is the same as for the single flat mold, as detailed above in the preceding section (*Single Flat Molds*) of this chapter. The upper half of the mold is constructed in a similar manner. Plywood is frequently used for making the mold surface. Cut the plywood to the desired size. Generally, this is slightly larger than the desired panel size and the same size or smaller than the lower section of the mold. The plywood should be larger than the largest desired size.

FORMING PANELS BY PRESSURE MOLDING

To pressure mold a flat panel in the double mold (Fig. 7-10), you will need a double flat mold, as detailed in the preceding section. You will need all the items on the materials list, plus cement building blocks for applying pressure to the upper mold surface.

The two sections of the flat mold are placed on the protective paper with the mold surfaces upward. Then apply a coat of the paste-type mold release, using a clean cloth to spread a thin layer of the release over the entire mold surface of each mold half. This is to keep the molding from sticking so that it can be removed after it has cured.

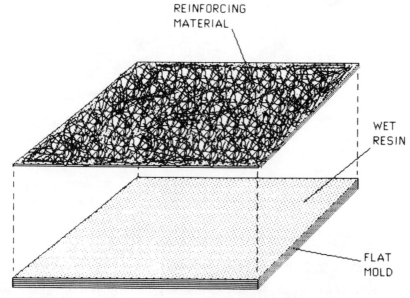

REINFORCING
MATERIAL

WET
RESIN

FLAT
MOLD

Fig. 7-3. First layer of reinforcing material is placed over wet resin.

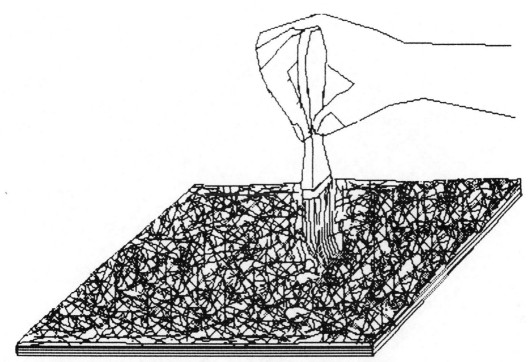

Fig. 7-4. A dabbing rather than brushing action is used to press fiberglass mat in place.

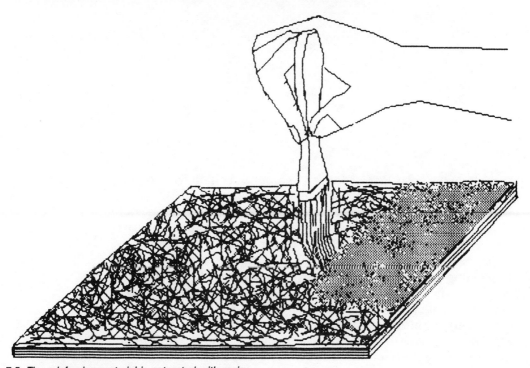

Fig. 7-5. The reinforcing material is saturated with resin.

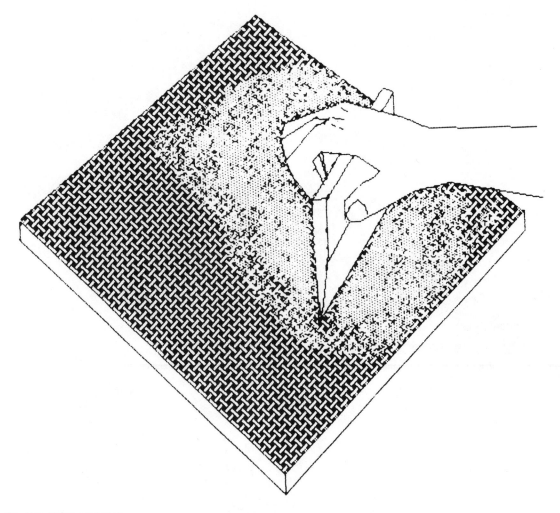

Fig. 7-6. Using squeegee.

Now follow the basic instructions in Chapter 6, beginning with Step 14. (Disregard Step 18.) Again refer to Figs. 7-3 through 7-9.

In Step 17, a double mold method is used, so all the layers should be laid up at once while wet. As a general rule, the maximum practical thickness for this method of molding is about 6 ounces of reinforcing material per square foot. After Step 27, don't clean the brush. Place the cement building block or blocks (more than one are required for larger mold areas) or other suitable weight on top of the upper half of the mold. Make sure that the upper half of the mold is level so that the laminate will have an equal thickness in all areas.

Allow the laminate to cure and remove it from the mold. It might be necessary to pry the laminate loose with a putty knife or other tool.

This completes the chemical part of the construction. Mark the pat-

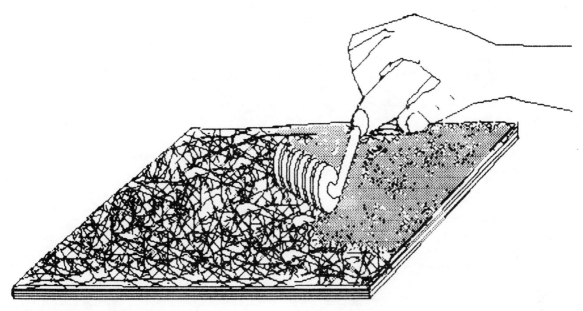

Fig. 7-7. Using laminating roller.

tern for the 10-inch square on the fiberglass molding and saw off excess laminate (about an inch all the way around).

File and sand the edges smooth. Polish and buff the gel coat surfaces and the edges of the laminate.

PROJECTS

Serving Tray

A serving tray (Fig. 7-11) combines fiberglass and wood construction to form a decorative and functional item. Use a 12-x-15-inch fiberglass panel of two layers of 1 1/2-ounce fiberglass mat with a layer of 10-ounce fiberglass cloth sandwiched between or equivalent thickness. (Fig. 7-12). The tray can also be made to other dimensions.

You can contact mold the panel with the smooth surface used for

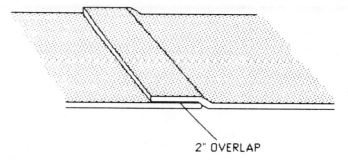

2" OVERLAP

Fig. 7-8. Reinforcing material joined with overlap.

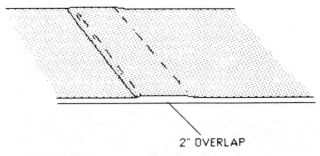

2" OVERLAP

Fig. 7-9. Mat overlap worked down to near even thickness.

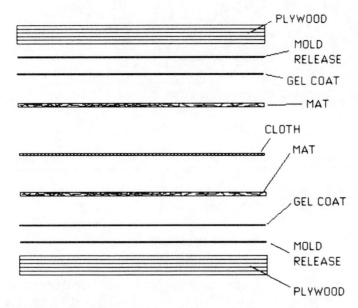

PLYWOOD

MOLD
RELEASE

GEL COAT

MAT

CLOTH

MAT

GEL COAT

MOLD
RELEASE

PLYWOOD

Fig. 7-10. Use of double mold to pressure mold flat panel with smooth surfaces on both sides.

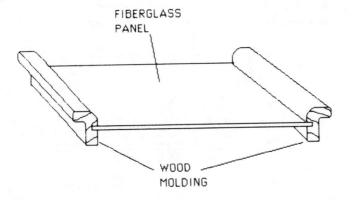

FIBERGLASS
PANEL

WOOD
MOLDING

Fig. 7-11. Serving tray.

112

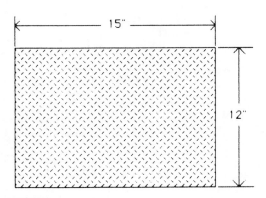

Fig. 7-12. Pattern for fiberglass panel.

the top of the tray or, better yet, double mold it so the bottom of the tray will also be smooth.

Regardless of whether a single or double mold is used, the appearance of the tray can be improved by laying down colored burlap or cotton cloth over a wet layer of resin applied to the gel coat in the mold before the first layer of fiberglass reinforcing material is added. Wash the material with a detergent and press it with a hot iron to remove all wrinkles before it is placed face down in the wet resin.

Make the end pieces from wood moldings (Fig. 7-13). Picture frame moldings with a notch for glass make construction easy, eliminating the need for making the notch for the fiberglass panel. You can use corner molding if you have the woodworking tools and skill to notch the wood (this can be done with a circular saw or router). Regardless, cut the wood pieces to length to match the width of the fiberglass panel and sand and finish as desired.

The front and back edges of the fiberglass tray panel should be rounded slightly and filed, sanded, and buffed smooth. The assembly of the wood end pieces and the fiberglass panel is shown in Fig. 7-14.

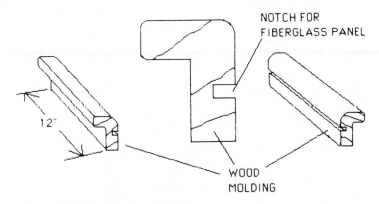

Fig. 7-13. End pieces made from wood moldings.

113

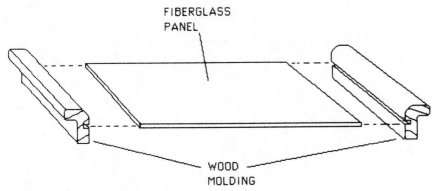

FIBERGLASS PANEL

WOOD MOLDING

Fig. 7-14. Assembly of serving tray.

Attach the fiberglass to the wood with epoxy glue or mechanical fasteners.

Wastebasket

You can make a wastebasket (Fig. 7-15) from a thin fiberglass panel of one layer of 10-ounce fiberglass cloth or one layer of 1-ounce fiberglass mat. Make the wastebasket to the dimensions you wish.

The panel can be contact molded with the smooth surface used for the outside of the wastebasket or double molded so that both the outside and inside of the wastebasket will be smooth.

The thin fiberglass panel is rolled and epoxy glued with a 1-inch overlap (Fig. 7-16).

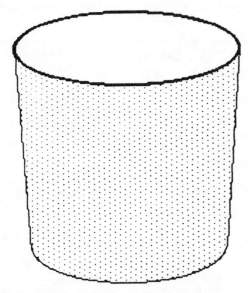

Fig. 7-15. Waste basket made from thin panel of fiberglass.

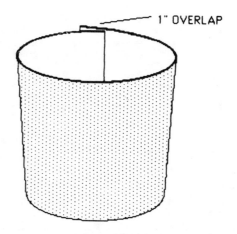

Fig. 7-16. Thin fiberglass panel is rolled and lap joint is epoxy glued.

The top and bottom edges of the fiberglass should be rounded slightly and filed, sanded, and buffed smooth. Cut the bottom of the wastebasket from 1/4-inch plywood and glue in place to the fiberglass with epoxy (Fig. 7-17).

Place Mat

You can make a place mat (Fig. 7-18) from a fiberglass panel of one layer of 1 1/2-ounce, 12- x -16-inch fiberglass mat or reinforcing material of equivalent thickness (Fig. 7-19). The place mat can also be made to other dimensions.

Contact mold the panel with the smooth surface used for the top

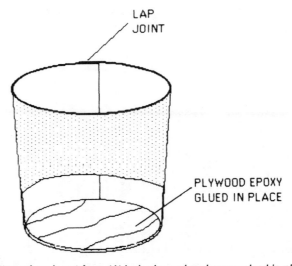

Fig. 7-17. Bottom piece is cut from 1/4-inch plywood and epoxy glued in place.

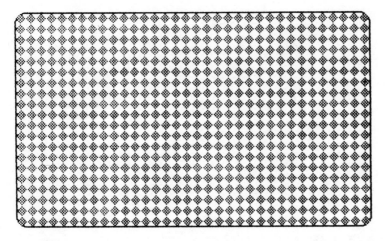

Fig. 7-18. Place mat.

of the place mat or double mold it so the bottom of the place mat will also be smooth.

Here again you may use colored burlap or cotton cloth. Lay it down over a wet layer of resin applied to the gel coat in the mold before the fiberglass reinforcing material is added. Wash and press the material, then place it face down in the wet resin.

The panel is cut to dimensions with rounded corners. The edges of the fiberglass place mat should be rounded slightly and filed, sanded, and buffed smooth.

Shade for Floor Lamp

A shade for a floor lamp (Fig. 7-20) combines fiberglass and wire construction. A thin, rectangular fiberglass panel of one layer of 10-ounce

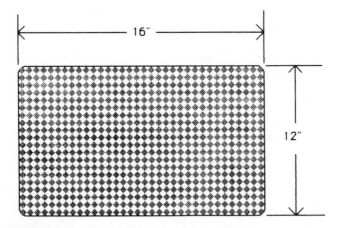

Fig. 7-19. Pattern for place mat.

116

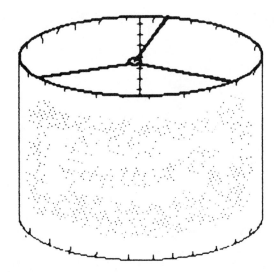

Fig. 7-20. Lampshade.

fiberglass cloth or 1-ounce fiberglass mat is required (Fig. 7-21). The shade can be made to desired dimensions.

Contact or double mold the panel.

The edges of the fiberglass lampshade panel should be rounded slightly and filed, sanded, and buffed smooth. Small holes are drilled 1 inch apart all the way around the fiberglass panel for wire lacing (Fig. 7-22). Lace the ends of the fiberglass panel together with small-diameter wire.

You can use wire lampshade wire rings and mounting wires from an old floor lamp lampshade, or you can form your own from wire. Lace these to the top and bottom edges of the shade with small-diameter wire.

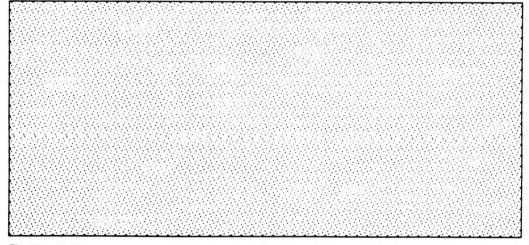

Fig. 7-21. A thin rectangular panel of fiberglass is used to form floor lampshade.

Fig. 7-22. Holes are drilled 1 inch apart around edges for wire lacings.

Shade for Table Lamp

A shade for a table lamp (Fig. 7-23) is a variation on the preceding project. Use one layer of 10-ounce fiberglass cloth or 1-ounce fiberglass mat cut to the pattern shown in Fig. 7-24. Holes are drilled 1 inch apart around the fiberglass panel for wire lacing (Fig. 7-25). The fiberglass panel is then laced together with small-diameter wire.

Cabinet Doors, Decorative Screens, and Room Dividers

Cabinet doors (Fig. 7-26), sliding cabinet doors (Fig. 7-27), folding screens (Fig. 7-28), and room dividers (Fig. 7-29) are projects that use decorative fiberglass panels. A fiberglass panel of two layers of 1 1/2-ounce fiberglass with a layer of 10-ounce fiberglass cloth sandwiched between

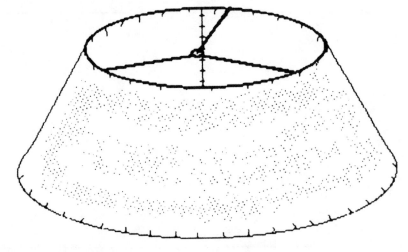

Fig. 7-23. Table lampshade.

118

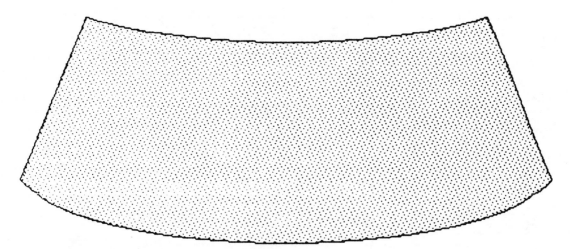

Fig. 7-24. Pattern for fiberglass panel for table lampshade.

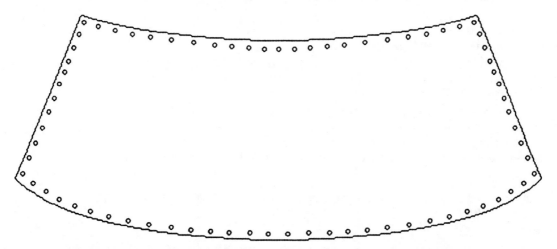

Fig. 7-25. Small holes are drilled 1 inch apart around edges of fiberglass panel for lacing wires.

Fig. 7-26. Cabinet door with decorative fiberglass panel.

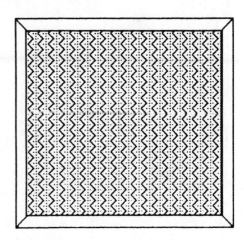

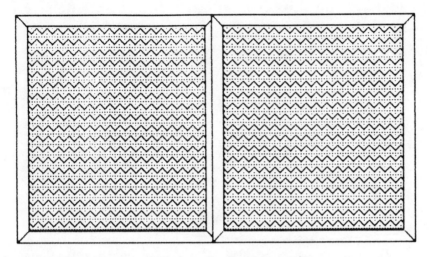

Fig. 7-27. Sliding cabinet doors with decorative fiberglass panels.

or equivalent thickness will suffice for areas up to about 2 square feet. Larger panels require thicker laminates.

The panels are double molded so that they have smooth surfaces on both sides. The appearance of the panels can be improved by laying down colored burlap or cotton cloth over a wet layer of resin applied to the gel coat in the mold before you add the first layer of fiberglass reinforcing material. Wash and press the material and place it face down in the wet resin.

The frames can be made from wood (Fig. 7-30) or aluminum (Fig.

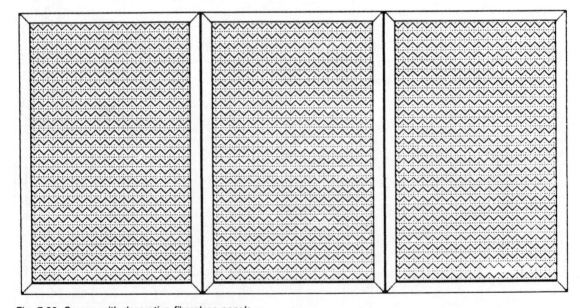

Fig. 7-28. Screen with decorative fiberglass panels.

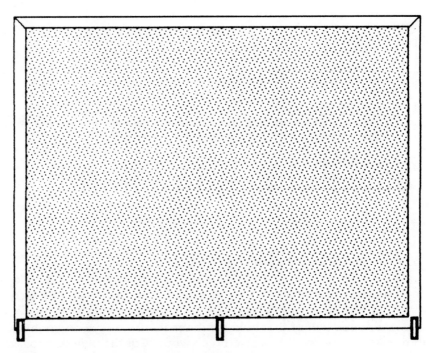

Fig. 7-29. Room divider with decorative fiberglass panel.

7-31) moldings. The base for the room divider can be constructed from wood (Fig. 7-32). Shape, sand, and finish the wood pieces as desired.

Fiberglass Tabletop

Fiberglass laminated to plywood makes an ideal decorative and protective tabletop for outdoor furniture (Fig. 7-33). Unlike the other projects using flat fiberglass panels detailed above, the laminate is bonded

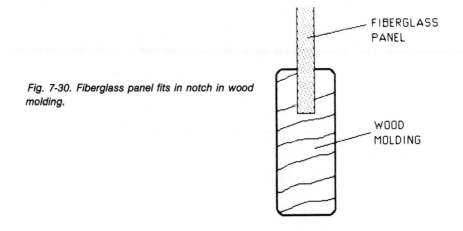

Fig. 7-30. Fiberglass panel fits in notch in wood molding.

FIBERGLASS PANEL

WOOD MOLDING

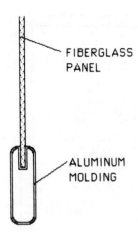

FIBERGLASS
PANEL

ALUMINUM
MOLDING

Fig. 7-31. Fiberglass panel fits in notch in aluminum molding.

directly to the plywood base (Fig. 7-34).

The plywood tabletop base used for the bottom half of the mold is the same as for the single flat mold, except that no release or gel coat will be applied, so the fiberglass is permanently bonded to the plywood base. The upper half of the mold can be made from plywood, which is cut to match the size of the tabletop plywood. Cut the plywood to size.

The plywood mold surface can be prepared by applying a thin coat of polyester resin and then sanding and polishing this to a smooth surface. Lacquer can be used in a similar manner. See the section on *Single Flat Molds* at the beginning of this chapter.

To pressure mold a layer of fiberglass mat to a plywood tabletop, you will need the upper half of a pressure mold, cement building blocks or other suitable weights for applying pressure to the upper mold surface (or C clamps to use around the edges to clamp the two pieces of wood together), a paste-type mold release, and the rest of the items on the materials list in Chapter 6.

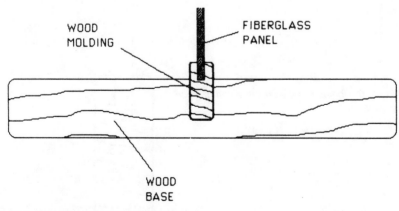

WOOD
MOLDING

FIBERGLASS
PANEL

WOOD
BASE

Fig. 7-32. Wood base for room divider.

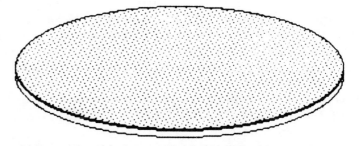

Fig. 7-33. Fiberglass pressure molded to plywood tabletop.

Place the upper section of the flat mold on the protective paper with the mold surfaces upward. Apply a coat of the paste-type mold release, using a clean cloth to spread a thin layer of the release over the entire mold surface. This will keep the molding from sticking so it can be removed after it has cured.

Now follow the basic instructions in Chapter 6, beginning with Step 14. (Disregard Step 18.)

In Step 20, you will probably need about 15 to 30 minutes of working time to apply the resin.

After completing Step 24, turn the upper half of the mold so that the cured gel coat surface is face down, and press it in place on top of the wet layer of mat before the laminate has had the chance to set up. Apply pressure downward and rock the upper section of the mold back and forth to work out any air. Then place the cement building block or

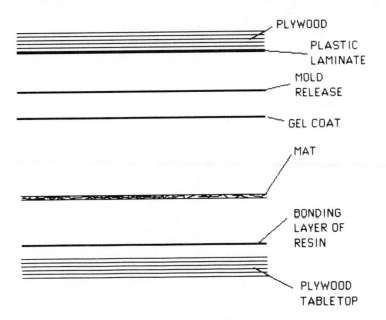

Fig. 7-34. Pressure molding a layer of fiberglass mat to plywood tabletop.

blocks (more than one are required for larger mold areas) or other suitable weight on top of the upper half of the mold. Make sure that the upper half of the mold is level so that the laminate will have an equal thickness in all areas. An alternate method is to use C clamps around the edge of the tabletop. Clean the resin from the brush with acetone before the resin hardens.

Allow the laminate to thoroughly cure. Then remove the upper mold half from it. Even though the mold release was used, it still may be necessary to pry the mold loose.

This completes the chemical part of the construction. Mark and saw off excess laminate so that the fiberglass is even with the edges of the plywood tabletop all the way around.

Next, file and sand the edges smooth. Polish and buff the gel coat surface of the fiberglass laminate.

The edges of the tabletop can be sealed with epoxy or covered with a plastic or metal molding. Use a sealing compound under the molding so that water will not work its way in.

Chapter 8

Projects for
Shallow Curved Molds

The projects up to this point have focused on flat molds. This is generally the best starting point, but the real creative fiberglass molding begins with curved surfaces.

All of the projects in this chapter require molding fiberglass to shallow curved shapes, with one or both surfaces against the mold surface. When one smooth surface is required, contact molding is used. When a molded surface is required on both sides of the object, pressure molding is used.

FORMING SHALLOW CURVED SHAPES BY CONTACT MOLDING

Basic methods for contact molding were introduced in Chapter 5.

Shallow Curved Molds

Contact molding gives a smooth surface on one side only, so it is important to note that there are two basic forms a shallow curved mold can take. If you want to mold a shallow curved dish with a smooth upper surface, the contact mold surface will look like the bottom surface of a bowl (Fig. 8-1). If you want to mold a shallow curved dish with a smooth under surface, the contact mold surface will look like the upper surface of a bowl (Fig. 8-2). To mold a shallow curved dish with a smooth upper surface, the mold is placed with the contact surface upward (see Fig. 8-1). The molding is then laid up over this (Fig. 8-3) and removed

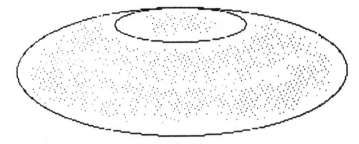

Fig. 8-1. Convex contact mold gives molding with smooth concave side.

from the mold after it has cured (Fig. 8-4). If it is to be used as a bowl, it is then turned over so that the smooth molded surface will be upward.

Contrast this to a mold for a shallow curved dish form with a smooth under surface (see Fig. 8-2). The mold is positioned like an upright bowl and the molding is laid up inside (Fig. 8-5) and removed from the mold after it has been cured (Fig. 8-6). Depending how the molding is to be used, it may be positioned like a bowl with a smooth underside or a cap with a smooth top. In each case, it is important to keep in mind that the molding is not a duplicate of the mold, but a reverse image. Duplication molding is the subject of a later chapter.

Now follow the basic instructions in Chapter 6, Steps 1 through 11.

In Step 1, a wood lathe is frequently used for shaping shallow curved molds from wood. Figure 8-7 shows a wood mold suitable for molding a shallow dish form with a smooth upper surface (when the bowl is turned upright). Figure 8-8 shows a wood mold suitable for molding a shallow dish form with a smooth lower surface (when the bowl is turned upright). Carving tools, surfacing tools, and files are useful for making irregular shallow curved forms.

In Step 6, refer to Fig. 8-9.

Contact Molding Shallow Curved Forms

To contact mold a shallow curved form, follow Steps 12 through 32 of the basic instructions in Chapter 6.

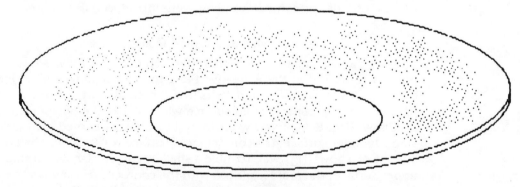

Fig. 8-2. Concave contact mold gives molding with smooth convex side.

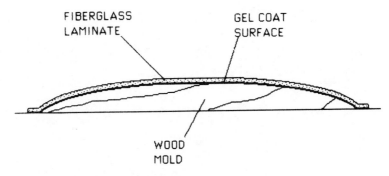

Fig. 8-3. Molding is laid up over convex mold form.

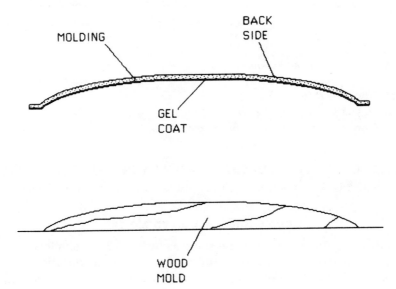

Fig. 8-4. Molding is removed from mold.

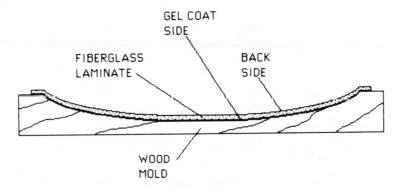

Fig. 8-5. Molding is laid up over concave mold form.

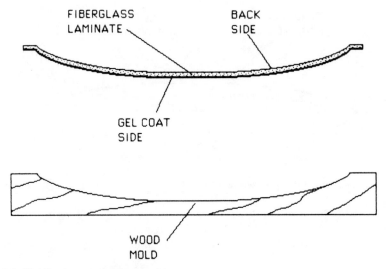

Fig. 8-6. Molding is removed from mold.

In Step 16, refer to Fig. 8-10.
In Step 23, refer to Fig. 8-11.
In Step 24, refer to Figs. 8-12 and 8-13.

FORMING SHALLOW CURVED SHAPES BY PRESSURE MOLDING

Basic methods for pressure molding were introduced in Chapter 5.

Double Shallow Curved Molds

The bottom half of the mold is the same as for the single shallow curved mold, as detailed above. For our purposes, we will consider the concave part of the mold as the bottom section and the convex part as the upper

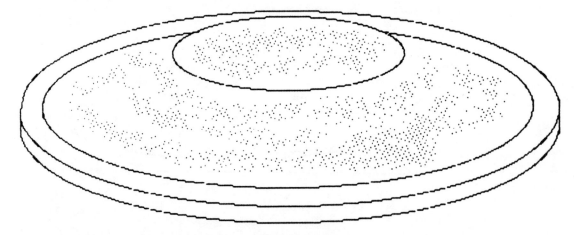

Fig. 8-7. Wood mold for laminating disk shape with smooth concave side.

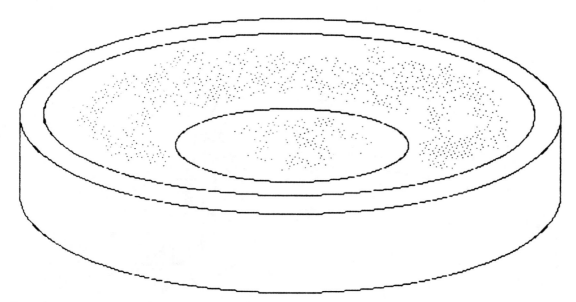

Fig. 8-8. Wood mold for laminating disk shape with smooth convex side.

Fig. 8-9. A smooth, thin layer of catalyzed polyester resin is brushed on wood molding surface.

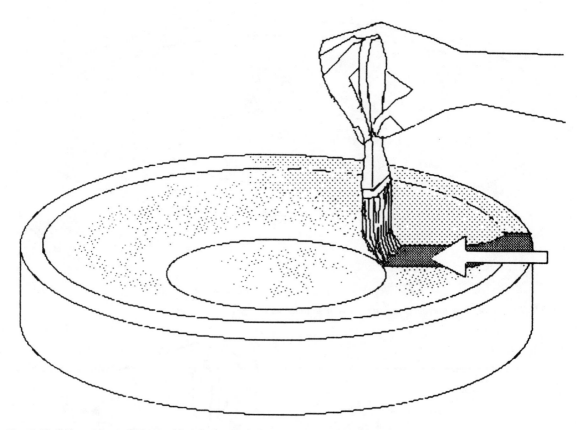

Fig. 8-10. Gel coat is applied to mold surface with long continuous strokes of brush.

section, because this is the position they are usually used for molding so that the resin will not run out of the mold (Fig. 8-14). The upper half of the mold matches the shape of the lower section (they fit together), except that space must be left for the molding. The space varies depending on the particular project, but 1/8 inch to 3/16 inch is typical.

Because pressure molding gives a smooth surface on both sides, it is important to have the two parts of the mold match each other, minus the desired thickness of the laminate. While the laminate does not necessarily have to be the same thickness throughout, varying the thickness can make molding much more difficult. All of the projects detailed in this chapter for shallow curved molds can be made with an even thickness of the laminate. The finished molding will have smooth surfaces on both sides, so it can be used like a bowl or cap, depending on the specific project you are making.

The upper or lower section of a shallow curved mold can be shaped from a single piece of wood, or two or more pieces can be glued together. You can use a wood lathe for shaping these molds from wood. Figure 8-8 shows a wood mold suitable for molding the bottom surface of a shallow dish form (when the bowl is turned upright). Figure 8-15 shows

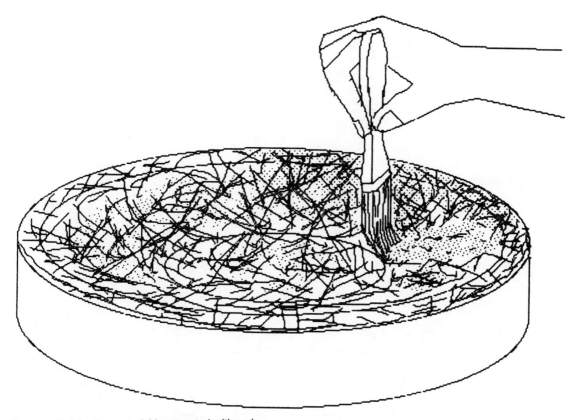

Fig. 8-11. Reinforcing material is saturated with resin.

the matching section of a wood mold suitable for molding the upper surface on inside of the dish form surface (when the bowl is turned upright). Carving tools, surfacing tools, and files are useful for making irregular shallow curved forms.

Now follow Steps 1 through 11 of the basic instructions.

In Step 6, refer back to Fig. 8-9.

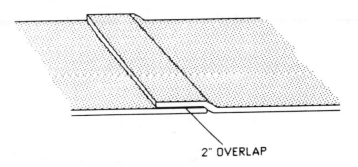

2" OVERLAP

Fig. 8-12. Reinforcing material joined with overlap.

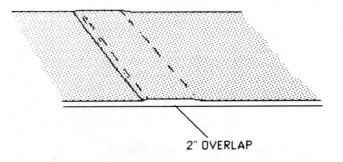

2" OVERLAP

Fig. 8-13. Mat overlap worked down to near even thickness.

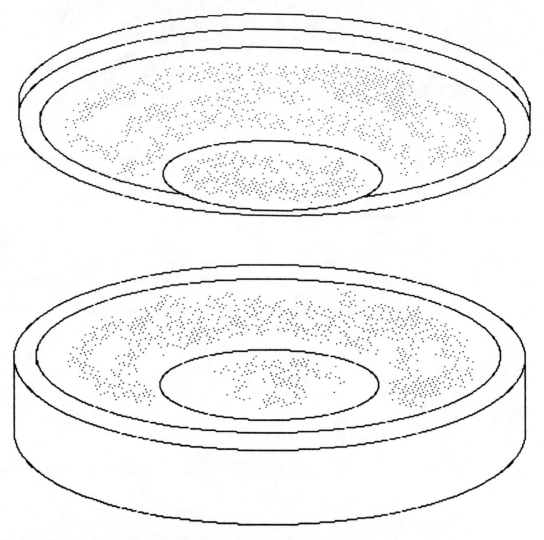

Fig. 8-14. Double mold for pressure molding shallow curved form.

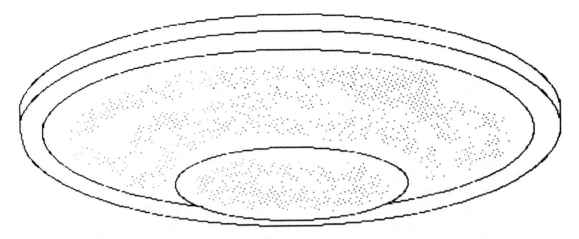

Fig. 8-15. Upper section of mold made from wood.

Pressure Molding Shallow Curved Forms

To pressure mold a shallow curved form in the double mold (Fig. 8-16), you will need the items on the materials list, plus a cement building block or other suitable weight for applying pressure to the upper mold surface or C clamps that can be used around the edges to hold the two mold parts together under pressure.

Now follow the basic instructions, Steps 12 through 32. (Disregard Step 24.)

After Step 27, turn the upper half of the mold before the laminate has the chance to set up, so that the cured gel coat surface is face down

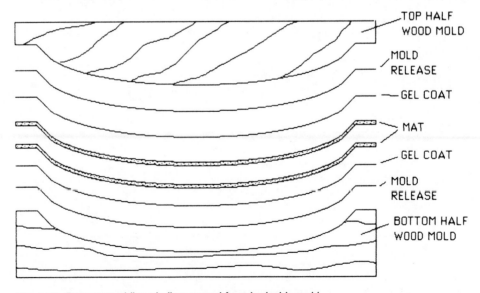

Fig. 8-16. Pressure molding shallow curved form in double mold.

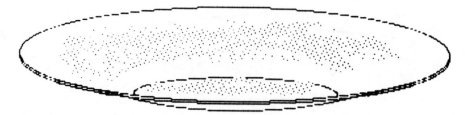

Fig. 8-17. Shallow curved dish.

and press it in place on top of the wet layer of fiberglass reinforcing material. Apply pressure downward and rock the upper section of the mold back and forth to work out any air. Then place the cement building block or blocks or other suitable weight on top of the upper half of the mold or use C clamps to hold the mold parts together. Make sure that the upper half of the mold is level so that the laminate will have an equal thickness in all areas.

Clean the brush. Go on to Steps 31 and 32.

PROJECTS

Shallow Curved Dish

The dish in Fig. 8-17 can be contact molded to give a smooth surface on one side only, or double molded to give a smooth surface on both sides. If contact molding is used, the upper or lower surface of the dish can be the smooth one, as desired.

The single or double mold can be shaped from wood as detailed previously in this chapter. Figure 8-18 shows dish shapes suitable for contact molding with the upper surface of the dish as the smooth side

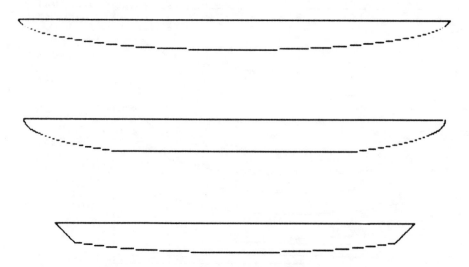

Fig. 8-18. Shallow dish shapes suitable for contact molding.

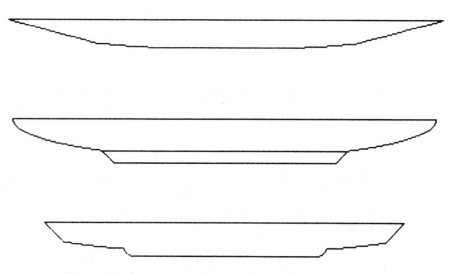

Fig. 8-19. Shallow dish shapes suitable for pressure molding.

(these will be molded upside down). Figure 8-19 shows dish shapes suitable for double molding.

The next step is to contact or pressure mold the dish, using the methods detailed previously in this chapter.

After the dish has cured, remove it from the mold. Saw off excess fiberglass from edges of laminate and file and sand edges smooth, rounding them slightly.

Fruit Bowl

A fruit bowl is shown in Fig. 8-20. A fiberglass laminate of two layers of 1 1/2-ounce fiberglass mat or equivalent thickness is usually adequate for a fruit bowl up to about 14 inches in diameter. Three layers or more layers of 1 1/2-ounce mat can be used for larger sizes.

Shape the double mold from wood to the pattern shown in Fig. 8-21,

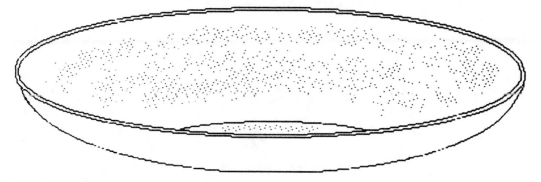

Fig. 8-20. Fruit bowl.

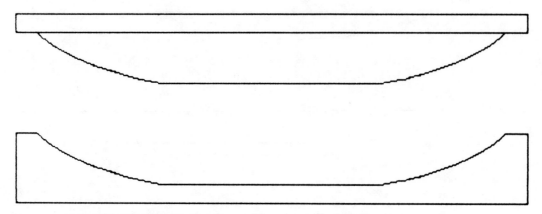

Fig. 8-21. Pattern for double mold for fruit bowl.

then pressure mold the fruit bowl using the methods detailed previously in this chapter.

After the dish has cured, remove it from the mold. Saw off excess fiberglass from edges of laminate and file and sand edges smooth, rounding them slightly.

Fig. 8-22. Table lamp with fiberglass shade.

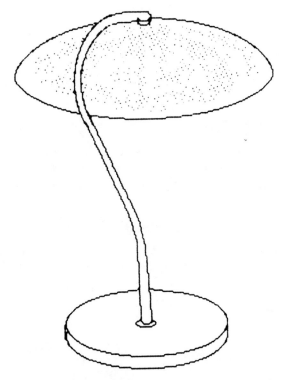

Fig. 8-23. Desk lamp with fiberglass shade.

These instructions may be followed for the rest of the projects in this chapter.

Table or Desk Lamp Shade

A table lamp shade is shown in Fig. 8-22 and a desk lamp shade in Fig. 8-23. A fiberglass laminate of two layers of 1 1/2-ounce fiberglass mat or equivalent thickness is usually adequate.

Shape the double mold from wood to the patten shown in Figure 8-24, then pressure mold the lap shade using the methods detailed previously in this chapter.

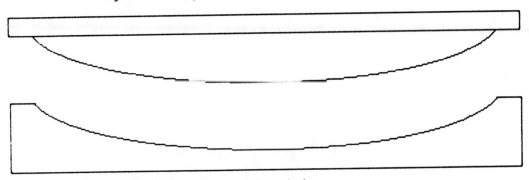

Fig. 8-24. Pattern for double mold for table or desk lamp shade.

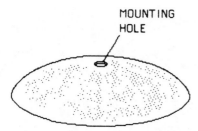

MOUNTING
HOLE

Fig. 8-25. Mounting hole is drilled in fiberglass lamp shade.

After the lamp shade molding has cured, remove it from the mold. Saw off excess fiberglass from edges of laminate and file and sand edges smooth, rounding them slightly. Drill mounting hole in center of shade (Fig. 8-25).

Bird Bath

A bird bath is shown in Fig. 8-26. A fiberglass laminate of three layers of 1 1/2-ounce fiberglass mat or equivalent thickness is usually adequate

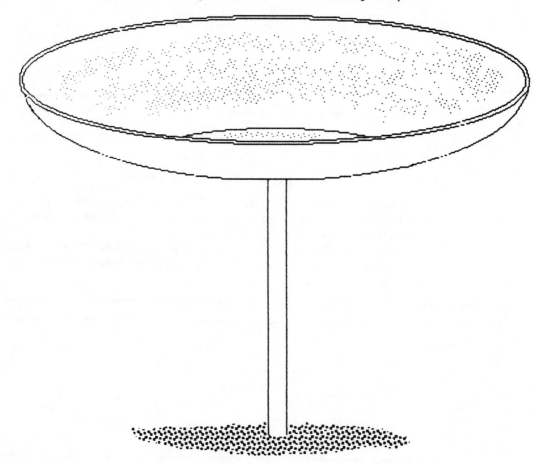

Fig. 8-26. Bird bath.

138

Fig. 8-27. Pattern for contact mold for bird bath pan.

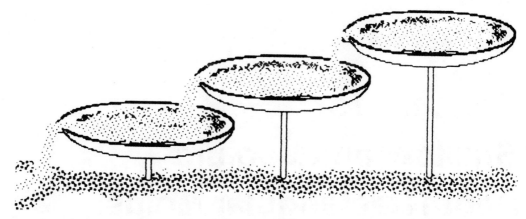

Fig. 8-28. Staircase waterfall made from fiberglass moldings.

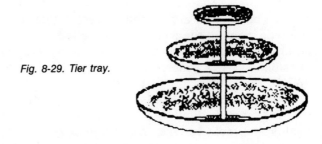

Fig. 8-29. Tier tray.

for a bird bath up to about 18 inches in diameter.

Figure 8-27 shows the pattern for a contact mold. The pattern is similar to Fig. 8-24, but the size is different. The molds can be shaped from wood, as detailed previously in this chapter.

Other Projects Using Shallow Curved Moldings

Using the same methods, a variety of other projects are possible, including a staircase waterfall fountain (Fig. 8-28) and a tier tray (Fig. 8-29). You will probably think of many other ways to use shallow curved moldings.

Chapter 9

Projects for Shallow and Medium-Depth Rectangular Molds

Included in this chapter are projects that have curved rectangular forms, such as bowls that are elongated rectangular designs. These projects combine many of the techniques detailed in Chapter 6 for flat molding and in Chapter 7 for shallow curved forms, adding many new creative possibilities. As a general rule, the molding becomes more difficult the greater the curves and/or the deeper the mold.

All of the projects in this chapter require molding fiberglass to shallow and medium-depth rectangular shapes, with one or both surfaces against the mold surface. When one smooth surface is required, contact molding is used. When a molded surface is required on both sides of the object, pressure molding is used.

FORMING SHALLOW AND MEDIUM-DEPTH RECTANGULAR SHAPES BY CONTACT MOLDING

Basic methods for contact molding were introduced in Chapter 5.

Shallow and Medium-Depth Rectangular Contact Molds

Because contact molding gives a smooth surface on one side only, there are two basic forms a shallow or medium-depth rectangular contact mold can take. If you want to mold a shallow rectangular tray with a smooth upper surface, the contact mold surface will look like the bottom surface of a tray (Fig. 9-1). If you want to mold a shallow rectangular tray

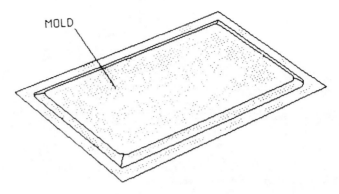

Fig. 9-1. Convex contact mold for tray form gives molding with smooth concave side.

with a smooth under surface, the contact mold surface will look like the upper surface of a tray (Fig. 9-2). To mold a shallow rectangular tray with a smooth upper surface, the mold is placed with the contact surface upward (see Fig. 9-1). The molding is then laid up over this (Fig. 9-3) and removed from the mold after it has cured (Fig. 9-4). If it is to be used as a tray, it is then turned over so that the smooth molded surface will be upward.

Contrast this to a mold for a shallow rectangular tray form with a smooth under surface (see Fig. 9-2). The mold is positioned like an upright tray and the molding is laid up inside (Fig. 9-5) and removed from the mold after it has been cured (Fig. 9-6). Depending how the molding is to be used, it can be positioned like a tray with a smooth underside or a cap or lid with a smooth top. Remember that the molding is not a duplicate of the mold, but a reverse image. Duplication molding is the subject of a later chapter.

Figure 9-7 shows a wood mold suitable for molding a shallow tray form with a smooth upper surface (when the tray is turned upright). Fig-

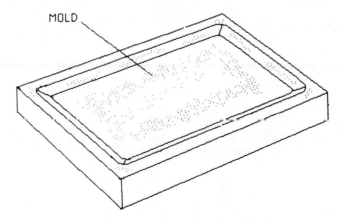

Fig. 9-2. Concave contact mold gives molding with smooth convex side.

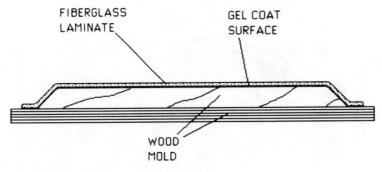

Fig. 9-3. Molding is laid up over convex mold form.

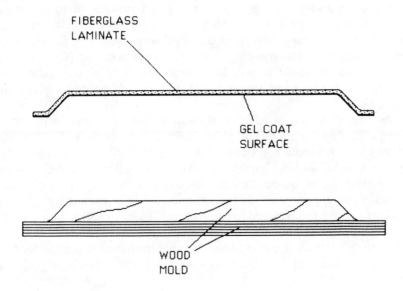

Fig. 9-4. Molding is removed from mold.

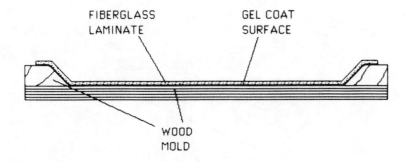

Fig. 9-5. Molding is laid up over concave mold form.

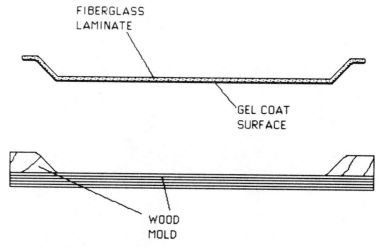

FIBERGLASS
LAMINATE

GEL COAT
SURFACE

WOOD
MOLD

Fig. 9-6. Molding is removed from mold.

ure 9-8 shows a wood mold suitable for molding a shallow tray form with
a smooth lower surface (when the tray is turned upright).

Now follow the basic instructions. Steps 1 through 11.

In Step 6, refer to Fig. 9-9.

Contact Molding Shallow and Medium-Depth Rectangular Forms. To
contact mold a shallow or medium depth rectangular form, follow Steps
12 through 32 in Chapter 6.

In Step 16, refer to Fig. 9-10.

In Step 23, refer to Fig. 9-11.

In Step 24, refer to Figs. 9-12 and 9-13.

FORMING SHALLOW AND MEDIUM-DEPTH
RECTANGULAR FORMS BY PRESSURE MOLDING

Basic methods for pressure molding were introduced in Chapter 5. We
will now expand on these.

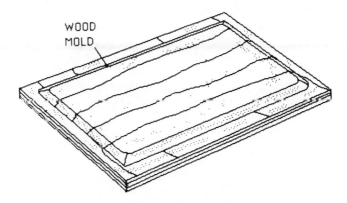

WOOD
MOLD

Fig. 9-7. Wood mold for laminating tray shape with smooth concave side.

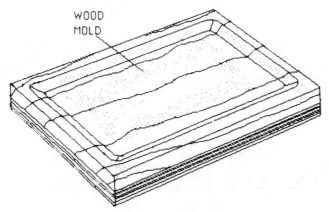

Fig. 9-8. Wood mold for contact molding tray form with smooth convex side.

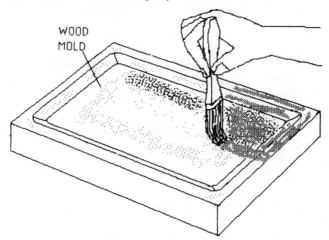

Fig. 9-9. A smooth, thin layer of catalyzed polyester resin is brushed on wood molding surface.

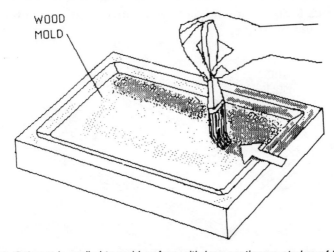

Fig. 9-10. Gel coat is applied to mold surface with long continuous strokes of brush.

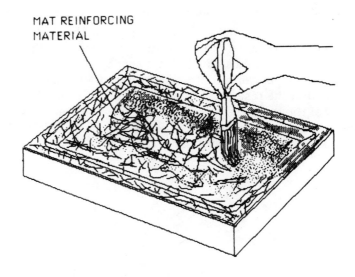

MAT REINFORCING
MATERIAL

Fig. 9-11. Reinforcing material is saturated with resin.

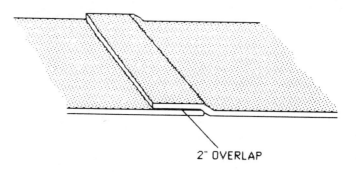

2" OVERLAP

Fig. 9-12. Reinforcing material joined with overlap.

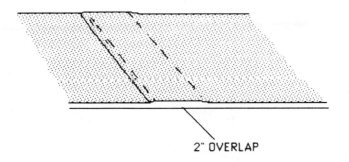

2" OVERLAP

Fig. 9-13. Mat overlap worked down to near even thickness.

Double Shallow and Medium-Depth Rectangular Molds

The bottom half of the mold is the same as for the single shallow or medium depth rectangular mold. For our purposes, we will consider the concave part of the mold as the bottom section and the convex part as the upper section. Because this is the position they are usually used for molding so that the resin does not run out of the mold (Fig. 9-14). The upper half of the mold matches the shape of the lower section (they fit together), except that space must be left for the molding. The space varies depending on the particular project, but 1/8 inch to 3/16 inch is typical.

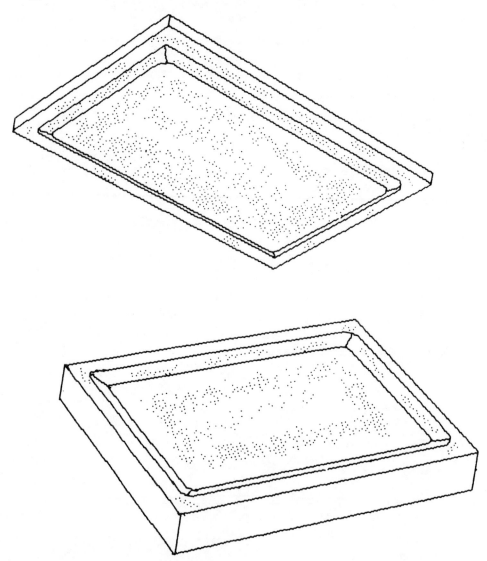

Fig. 9-14. Double mold for pressure molding tray form.

Because pressure molding gives a smooth surface on both sides, it is important to have the two parts of the mold match each other, minus the desired thickness of the laminate. While the laminate does not necessarily have to be the same thickness throughout, varying the thickness can make molding much more difficult. All of the projects detailed in this chapter for shallow and medium depth rectangular molds can be made with an even thickness of the laminate. Because the finished molding will have smooth surfaces on both sides, it can be used like a pan or lid, depending on the specific project you are making.

Refer back to Fig. 9-8 which shows a wood mold suitable for molding the bottom surface of a shallow tray form (when the tray is turned upright). Figure 9-15 shows the matching section of a wood mold suitable for molding the upper surface on inside of the tray form surface (when the tray is turned upright).

Now follow Steps 1 through 11 in Chapter 6. Keep in mind that, with pressure molding, you will be concerned with both the concave and convex molding forms. With these rectangular forms, the main problem is finding two mold halves that match.

Pressure Molding Shallow and Medium-Depth Rectangular Forms. To pressure mold a shallow or medium-depth rectangular form in the double mold (Fig. 9-16), you will need, in addition to the items on the materials list, a cement building block or other suitable weight for applying pressure to the upper mold surface or C clamps that can be used around the edges to hold the two mold parts together under pressure.

Now follow Steps 12 through 32 in Chapter 6.

In Step 17, laminate the first layer of fiberglass reinforcing material to the gel coat of the bottom half of the double mold.

In Step 23, refer back to Fig. 9-11. Skip Step 24.

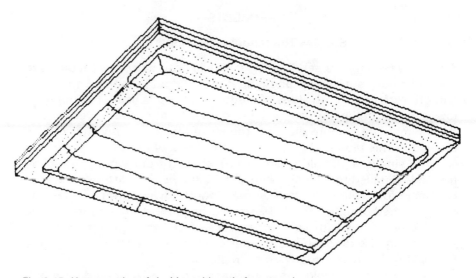

Fig. 9-15. Upper section of double mold made from wood.

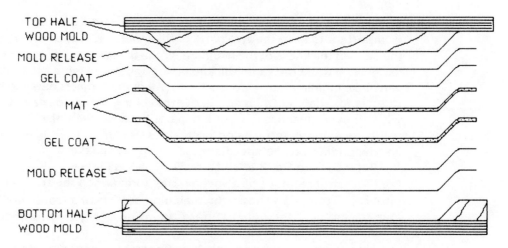

TOP HALF
WOOD MOLD

MOLD RELEASE

GEL COAT

MAT

GEL COAT

MOLD RELEASE

BOTTOM HALF
WOOD MOLD

Fig. 9-16. Pressure molding tray form in double mold.

After completing Step 26, apply all layers of reinforcing material that are to be used at this time. Before the laminate has had a chance to set up, turn the upper half of the mold so that the cured gel coat surface is face down and press it in place on top of the wet layer of fiberglass reinforcing material. Apply pressure downward and rock the upper section of the mold back and forth to work out any air. Then place the cement building block or blocks or other suitable weight on top of the upper half of the mold or use C clamps to hold the mold parts together under pressure. Make sure that the upper half of the mold is level so that the laminate will have an equal thickness in all areas. Clean the brush. Go on to Step 31 and 32.

PROJECTS

Shallow Rectangular Serving Tray

A shallow rectangular serving tray (Fig 9-17) can be contact molded to give a smooth surface on one side only, or double molded to give a smooth surface on both sides. If contact molding is used, the upper or lower surface of the tray can be the smooth side, as desired. Even though double molding is more difficult, the more attractive tray that can be molded in this manner is well worth the extra effort.

The single or double mold can be shaped from wood, using the methods detailed previously. Figure 9-18 shows the pattern for a contact mold for making the tray with a smooth lower surface (when the tray is turned upright); Fig. 9-19 shows the pattern for a contact mold for making the tray with a smooth upper surface (when the tray is turned upright); and Fig. 9-20 shows the pattern for a two-part pressure mold for making the tray smooth on both sides.

After a suitable mold has been constructed and prepared for mold-

Fig. 9-17. Shallow rectangular serving tray.

Fig. 9-18. Pattern for wood mold for contact molding rectangular tray with smooth lower surface.

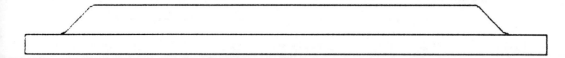

Fig. 9-19. Pattern for wood mold for contact molding rectangular tray with smooth upper surface.

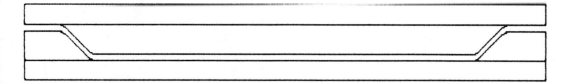

Fig. 9-20. Pattern for double mold for shallow rectangular tray.

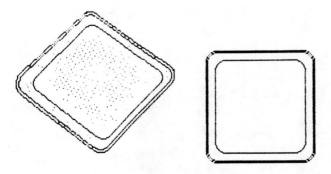

Fig. 9-21. Shallow square serving tray.

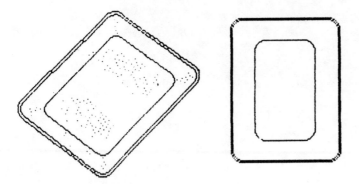

Fig. 9-22. Medium-depth rectangular tray.

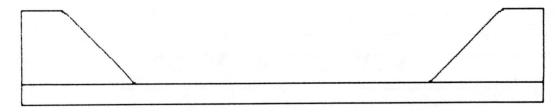

Fig. 9-23. Pattern for wood mold for contact molding medium-depth rectangular tray with smooth lower surface.

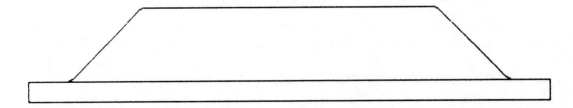

Fig. 9-24. Pattern for wood mold for contact molding medium-depth rectangular tray with smooth upper surface.

150

Fig. 9-25. Pattern for double mold for medium-depth rectangular tray.

ing, contact or pressure mold the tray. You can add decorative cloth fabric to the upper flat surface of the laminate. This is applied in the mold over a wet layer of resin applied over the gel coat resin.

After the tray laminate has cured, remove it from the mold. Saw off excess fiberglass from edges of laminate and file and sand edges smooth, rounding them slightly.

These instructions may be followed for the rest of the projects in this chapter.

Shallow Square Serving Tray

A shallow square serving tray is shown in Fig. 9-21.

Refer back to Figs. 9-18, 9-19, and 9-20 for illustrations of these molds. The only difference is that here you are working with squares rather than rectangles.

Medium-Depth Rectangular Tray

A medium-depth rectangular tray is shown in Fig. 9-22.

Figure 9-23 shows the pattern for a contact mold for making the tray with a smooth lower surface (when the tray is turned upright); Fig. 9-24 shows the pattern for a contact mold for making the tray with a smooth upper surface (when the tray is turned upright); and Fig. 9-25 shows the

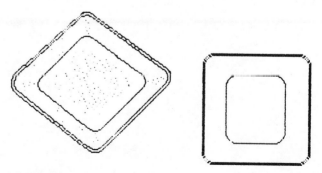

Fig. 9-26. Medium-depth square tray.

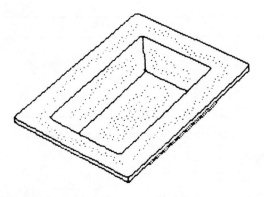

Fig. 9-27. Ash tray.

pattern for a two-part pressure mold for making the tray smooth on both sides.

Medium-Depth Square Tray

A medium-depth square tray is shown in Fig. 9-26.

Refer back to Figs. 9-23, 9-24, and 9-25. The only difference is that here you are working with squares rather than rectangles.

Other Projects Using Shallow Curved Moldings

Using the same methods detailed above, a variety of other projects are possible using the same basic molding form, including ash trays (Fig. 9-27), desk lampshades, and decorative pans.

Chapter 10

Projects for Medium-Depth and Deep Round Molds

Projects using single or double medium depth and deep round molds include lamp shades, planters, and bowls. As a general rule, the molding becomes more difficult the greater the curves and/or the deeper the mold.

All of the projects detailed in this chapter require molding fiberglass to medium-depth and deep round shapes, with one or both surfaces against the mold surface. When one smooth surface is required, contact molding is used. When a molded surface is required on both sides of the object, pressure molding is used.

FORMING MEDIUM-DEPTH AND DEEP ROUND SHAPES BY CONTACT MOLDING

Basic methods for contact molding shallow round shapes were introduced in Chapter 8.

Medium-Depth and Deep Round Contact Molds

Shallow and medium-depth round contact molds are frequently shaped on a wood lathe. Because contact molding gives a smooth surface on one side only, there are two basic forms a medium-depth or deep round contact mold can take. If you want to mold a cylindrical cone with a smooth inside surface, the contact mold surface will look like the outside of an upside down cone (Fig. 10-1). If you want to mold a cylindri-

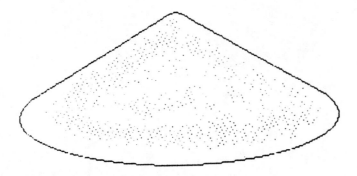

Fig. 10-1. Convex contact mold gives molding with smooth concave side.

cal cone with a smooth outside surface, the contact mold surface will look like the inside of a cone-shaped container (Fig. 10-2). To mold a cylindrical cone with a smooth inside surface, the mold is placed with the contact surface upward (see Fig. 10-1). The molding is then laid up over this (Fig. 10-3) and removed from the mold after it has cured (Fig. 10-4).

Contrast this to a mold for a cylindrical cone form with a smooth outside surface (see Fig. 10-2). The mold is positioned like an upright bowl and the molding is laid up inside (Fig. 10-5) and removed from the mold after it has been cured (Fig. 10-6). Depending how the molding is to be used, it may be positioned like a bowl with a smooth underside or a cap or lid with a smooth top. In each case, it is important to keep in mind that the molding is not a duplicate of the mold, but a reverse image. Duplication molding is the subject of a later chapter.

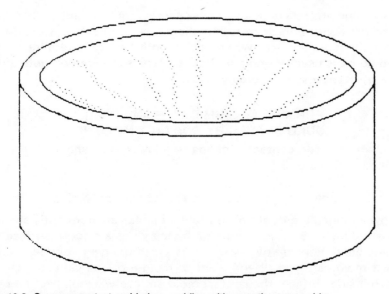

Fig. 10-2. Concave contact mold gives molding with smooth convex side.

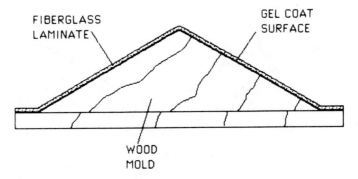

Fig. 10-3. Molding is laid up over convex mold form.

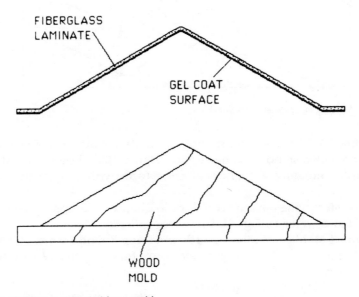

Fig. 10-4. Molding is removed from mold.

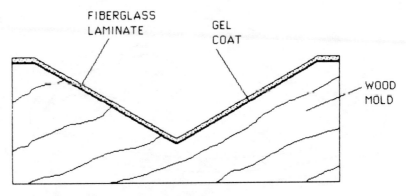

Fig. 10-5. Molding is laid up in concave mold form.

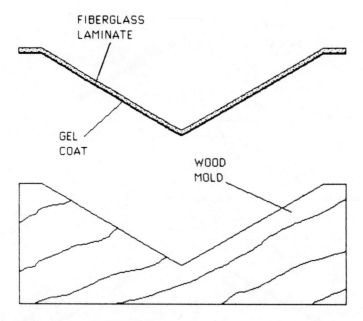

FIBERGLASS
LAMINATE

GEL
COAT

WOOD
MOLD

Fig. 10-6. Molding is removed from mold.

Figure 10-7 shows a wood mold suitable for molding a cylindrical cone form with a smooth inside surface. Figure 10-8 shows a wood mold suitable for molding a cylindrical cone form with a smooth outside surface.

Now refer to the basic instructions in Chapter 6, Steps 1 through 11.
In Step 6, refer to Fig. 10-9.

Contact Molding Medium-Depth and Deep Round Forms. To contact mold a medium-depth or deep round form, follow Steps 12 through 32 in Chapter 6.

In Step 16, refer to Fig. 10-10.
In Step 23, refer to Figs. 10-11, 10-12, 10-13.

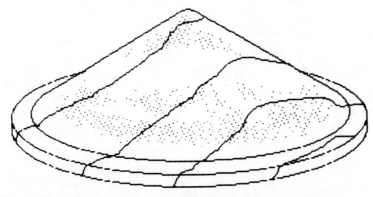

Fig. 10-7. Wood mold for laminating cone shape with smooth concave side.

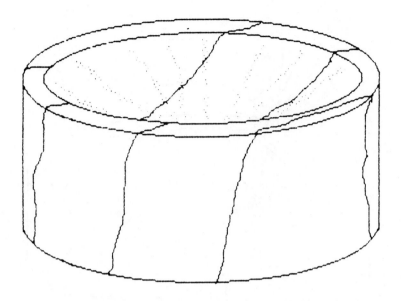

Fig. 10-8. Wood mold for laminating cone shape with smooth convex surface.

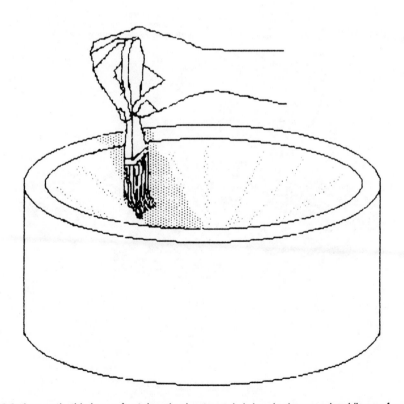

Fig. 10-9. A smooth, thin layer of catalyzed polyester resin is brushed on wood molding surface.

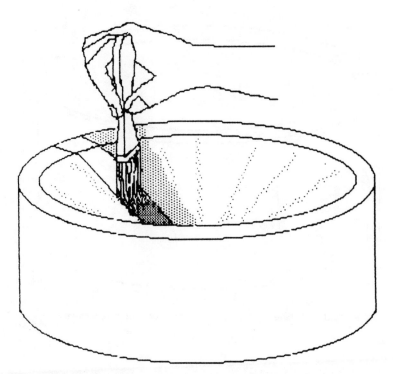

Fig. 10-10. Gel coat is applied to mold surface with long continuous strokes of brush.

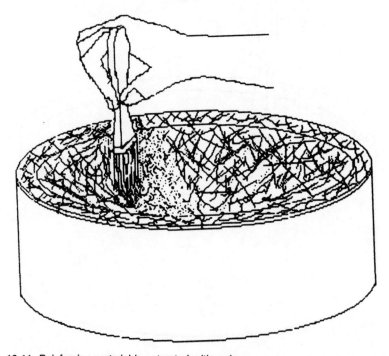

Fig. 10-11. Reinforcing material is saturated with resin.

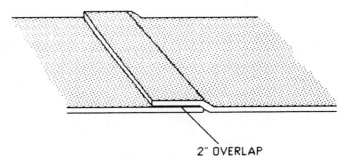

2" OVERLAP

Fig. 10-12. Reinforcing material joined with overlap.

FORMING MEDIUM-DEPTH AND
DEEP ROUND FORMS BY PRESSURE MOLDING

Basic methods for pressure molding shallow round forms were introduced in Chapter 8.

Medium-Depth and Deep Round Double Molds

The bottom half of the mold is the same as for the single medium-depth or deep round mold. We will consider the concave part of the mold as the bottom section and the convex part as the upper section, since this is the position they are usually used for molding so the resin does not run out of the mold (Fig. 10-14). The upper half of the mold matches the shape of the lower section (they fit together), except that space must be left for the molding. The space varies depending on the particular project, but 1/8 inch to 3/16 inch is typical.

The two parts of the mold match each other, minus the desired thickness of the laminate. While the laminate does not necessarily have to be the same thickness throughout, varying the thickness can make molding much more difficult. All of the projects detailed in this chapter for medium-depth and deep round molds can be made with an even thickness of the laminate. The finished molding will have smooth surfaces on both sides, so it can be used like a bowl or lid, depending on the specific project you are making.

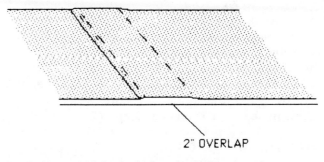

2" OVERLAP

Fig. 10-13. Mat overlap worked down to near even thickness.

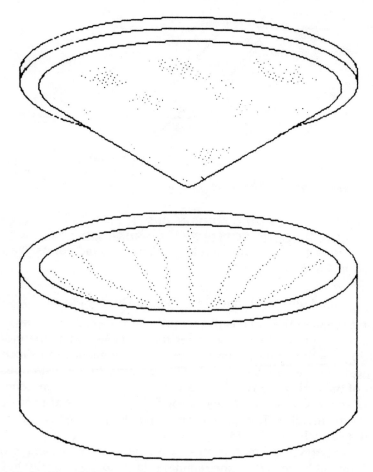

Fig. 10-14. Double mold for pressure molding cone form.

Figure 10-8 shows a wood mold suitable for molding the outside surface of a cylindrical cone form. Figure 10-15 shows the matching section of a wood mold suitable for molding the inside surface of the cylindrical cone form.

Now follow the basic instructions in Chapter 6, Steps 1 through 11.

In Step 6, refer to Fig. 10-9.

Pressure Molding Medium-Depth and Deep Round Forms. To pressure mold a medium-depth or deep round form in the double mold (Fig. 10-16), you will need the items on the materials list, plus a cement building block or other suitable weight for applying pressure to the upper mold surface or C clamps that can be used around the edges to hold the two mold parts together under pressure.

Now follow the basic instructions, Steps 12 through 32. (Disregard Step 24.)

In Step 23, refer to Fig. 10-11.

In Step 27, before the laminate has had a chance to set up, turn the

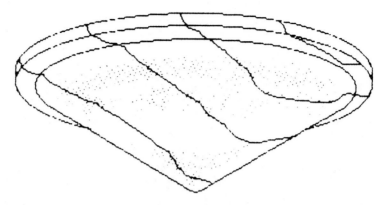

Fig. 10-15. Upper section of mold made from wood.

upper half of the mold so that the cured gel coat surface is face down and press it in place on top of the wet layer of fiberglass reinforcing material. Apply pressure downward and rock the upper section of the mold back and forth to work out any air. Then place the cement building block or blocks or other suitable weight on top of the upper half of the mold, or use C clamps to hold the mold parts together under pressure. Make sure that the upper half of the mold is level so that the laminate will

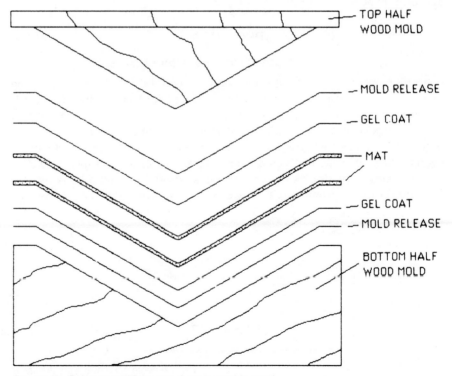

Fig. 10-16. Pressure molding cone form in double mold.

Fig. 10-17. Medium-depth cylindrical cone planter.

have an equal thickness in all areas. Clean the resin from the brush with acetone. Proceed to Steps 31 and 32.

PROJECTS

Medium-Depth Cylindrical Cone Planter

A medium-depth cylindrical cone planter (Fig. 10-17) is an interesting project. The cylindrical cone can be contact molded to give a smooth surface on one side only, or double molded to give a smooth surface on both sides. If contact molding is used, the inside or outside surface of the cone can be the smooth side, as desired. Even though double molding is more difficult, it gives a more attractive end product.

The single or double mold can be shaped from wood, using the methods detailed previously in this chapter. Figure 10-18 shows the pat-

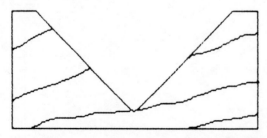

Fig. 10-18. Pattern for wood mold for contact molding medium-depth cone with smooth outside surface.

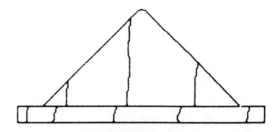

Fig. 10-19. Pattern for wood mold for contact molding medium-depth cone with smooth inside surface.

tern for a contact mold for making the cone with a smooth outside surface; Fig. 10-19 shows the pattern for a contact mold for making the cone with a smooth inside surface; and Fig. 10-20 shows the pattern for a two-part pressure mold for making the cone smooth both inside and outside.

After a suitable mold has been constructed and prepared for molding, contact or pressure mold the cone.

After the cone laminate has cured, remove it from the mold. Saw off excess fiberglass from edges of laminate and file and sand edges smooth, rounding them slightly. (These instructions may be followed for the rest of the projects in this chapter.)

Finish the planter by making a suitable stand from metal rod stock, wood, or other suitable material.

Medium-Depth Round Bowl

A medium-depth round bowl is shown in Fig. 10-21.

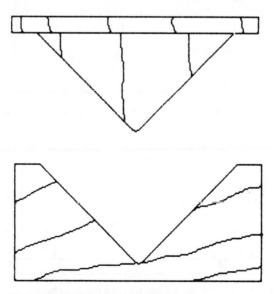

Fig. 10-20. Pattern for double mold for medium-depth cone.

Fig. 10-21. Medium-depth round bowl.

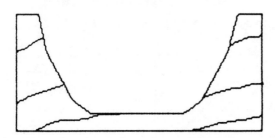

Fig. 10-22. Pattern for wood mold for contact molding medium-depth bowl with smooth outside surface.

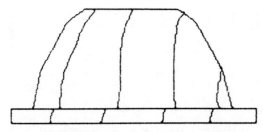

Fig. 10-23. Pattern for wood mold for contact molding medium-depth bowl with smooth inside surface.

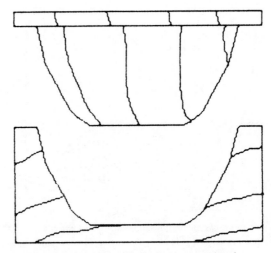

Fig. 10-24. Pattern for double mold for medium-depth round bowl.

The single or double mold can be shaped from wood. Figure 10-22 shows the pattern for a contact mold for making the bowl with a smooth outside surface; Fig. 10-23 shows the pattern for a contact mold for making the bowl with a smooth inside surface; and Fig. 10-24 shows the pat-

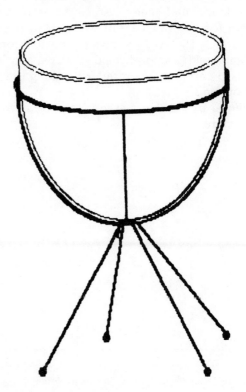

Fig. 10-25. Deep cylindrical planter.

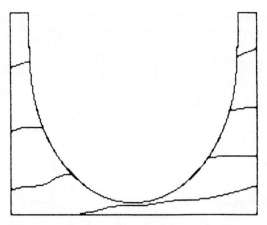

Fig. 10-26. Pattern for wood mold for contact molding cylindrical planter with smooth outside surface.

tern for a two-part pressure mold for making the bowl smooth both inside and outside.

Deep Cylindrical Planter

A deep cylindrical planter is shown in Fig. 10-25.

The single or double mold can be shaped from wood. Figure 10-26 shows the pattern for a contact mold for making the planter with a smooth outside surface; Fig. 10-27 shows the pattern for a contact mold for making the planter with a smooth inside surface; and Fig. 10-28 shows the pattern for a two-part pressure mold for making the planter smooth both inside and outside.

Finish the planter by making a stand from metal rod stock, wood, or other suitable material.

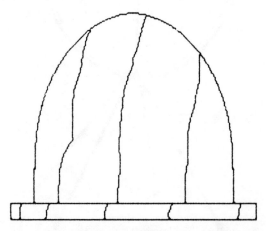

Fig. 10-27. Pattern for wood mold for contact molding deep cylindrical planter with smooth inside surface.

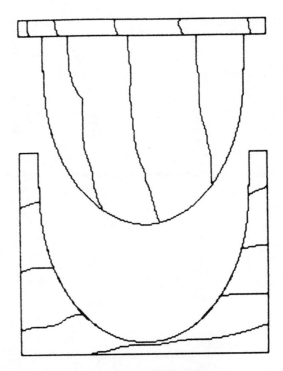

Fig. 10-28. Pattern for double mold for deep cylindrical planter.

Deep Round Lamp Shade

A deep round lamp shade, shown in Fig. 10-29, can be contact molded to give a smooth surface on one side only, or double molded to give a smooth surface on both sides.

The single or double mold can be shaped from wood. Figure 10-30 shows the pattern for a contact mold for making the lamp shade with a smooth outside surface; Fig. 10-31 shows the pattern for a contact mold for making the shade with a smooth inside surface (this would normally only be done if a rustic outside surface is desired); and Fig. 10-32 shows

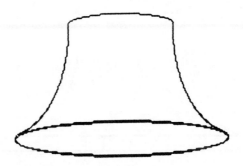

Fig. 10-29. Deep round lamp shade.

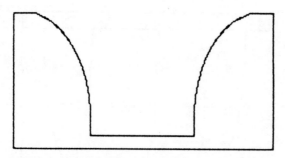

Fig. 10-30. Pattern for wood mold for contact molding deep round lamp shade with smooth outside surface.

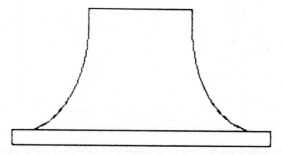

Fig. 10-31. Pattern for wood mold for contact molding deep round lamp shade with smooth inside surface.

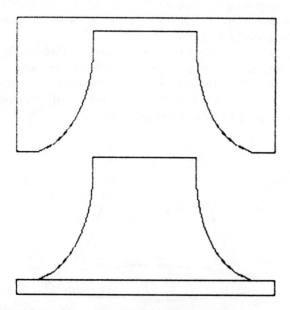

Fig. 10-32. Pattern for double mold for deep round lamp shade.

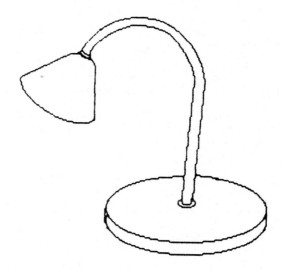

Fig. 10-33. Medium-depth cylindrical desk lamp shade.

the pattern for a two-part pressure mold for making the shade smooth both inside and outside.

Make wire mounting bracket and epoxy bond to inside of upper surface of lamp shade.

Other Projects Using Medium-Depth and Deep Round Moldings

Using the same methods detailed above, a variety of other projects are

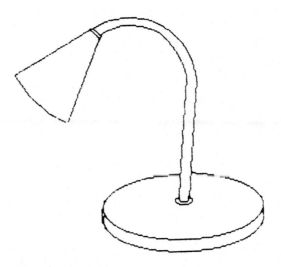

Fig. 10-34. Deep cylindrical desk lamp shade.

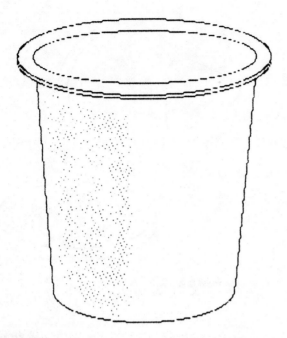

Fig. 10-35. Wastebasket.

possible using the same basic molding form, including medium-depth cylindrical desk lamp (Fig. 10-33), a deep cylindrical desk lamp (Fig. 10-34), and wastebasket (Fig. 10-35).

Chapter 11

Projects for Deep Rectangular Molds

Projects in this chapter using single or double deep rectangular molds include planters, boxes, cases, toy car bodies, and wagons. As a general rule, the molding is more difficult the greater the curves and/or the deeper the mold.

All of the projects require molding fiberglass to deep rectangular (with or without curved areas) shapes, with one or both surfaces against the mold surface. When one smooth surface is required, contact molding is used. When a molded surface is required on both sides of the object, pressure molding is used. With deep rectangular shapes, pressure or double molding is usually only practical with reasonably small moldings. In most cases, larger moldings should be contact molded.

FORMING DEEP RECTANGULAR SHAPES BY CONTACT MOLDING

Basic methods for contact molding shallow and medium depth rectangular shapes were covered in Chapter 9. We will now expand on these to include deep molds.

Deep Rectangular Contact Molds

Because contact molding gives a smooth surface on one side only, there are two basic forms a deep rectangular contact mold can take. If you want to mold a box shape with a smooth inside surface, the contact mold surface will look like the outside of an upside down box (Fig. 11-1). If

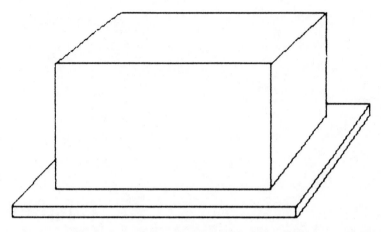

Fig. 11-1. Convex contact mold for box form gives molding with smooth concave or inside surface.

you want to mold a box shape with a smooth outside surface, the contact mold surface will look like the inside of a box with an open top (Fig. 11-2). To mold a box with a smooth inside surface, the mold is placed with the contact surface upward (Fig. 11-1). The molding is then laid up over this (Fig. 11-3) and removed from the mold after it has cured (Fig. 11-4).

Contrast this to a mold for a box form with a smooth outside surface (Fig. 11-2). The mold is positioned like an upright box with an open top and the molding is laid up inside (Fig. 11-5) and removed from the mold after it has been cured (Fig. 11-6). Depending how the molding is to be used, it may be positioned like a pan with a smooth underside and outsides or a cap or lid with a smooth top and outsides. In each case, it is important to keep in mind that the molding is not a duplicate of the mold, but a reverse image. Duplication molding is the subject of a later chapter.

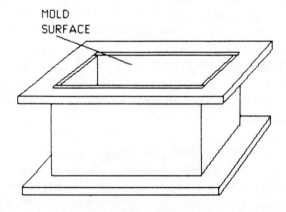

MOLD
SURFACE

Fig. 11-2. Concave contact mold gives box molding with smooth convex side or outside surface.

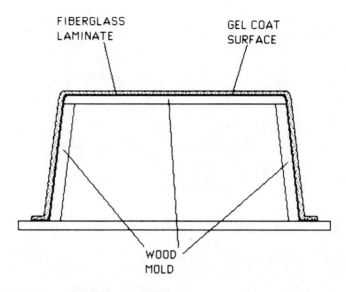

FIBERGLASS LAMINATE

GEL COAT SURFACE

WOOD MOLD

Fig. 11-3. Molding is laid up over convex mold form.

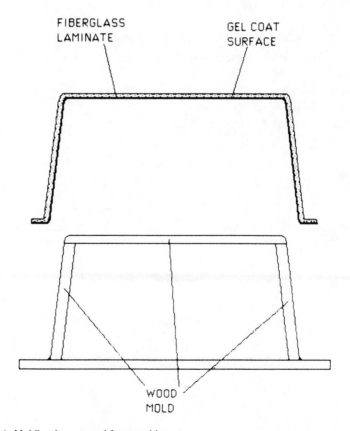

FIBERGLASS LAMINATE

GEL COAT SURFACE

WOOD MOLD

Fig. 11-4. Molding is removed from mold.

173

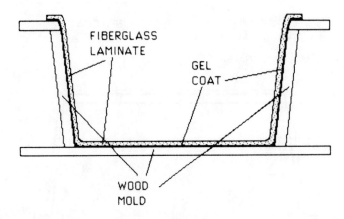

FIBERGLASS LAMINATE

GEL COAT

WOOD MOLD

Fig. 11-5. Molding is laid up over concave mold form.

Figure 11-7 shows a wood mold suitable for molding a box form with a smooth inside surface. Figure 11-8 shows a wood mold suitable for molding a box form with a smooth outside surface.

Now follow the basic instructions in Chapter 6, Steps 1 through 11.
In Step 6, refer to Fig. 11-9.

Contact Molding Deep Rectangular Forms

To contact mold a deep rectangular form, follow the basic instructions. Steps 12 through 32.

In Step 16, refer to Fig. 11-10.
In Step 23, refer to Fig. 11-11.
In Step 24, refer to Figs. 11-12, 11-13.

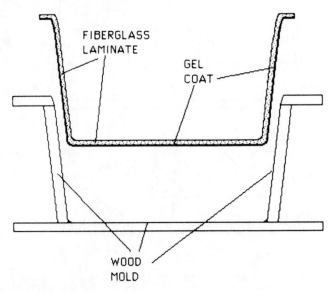

FIBERGLASS LAMINATE

GEL COAT

WOOD MOLD

Fig. 11-6. Molding is removed from mold.

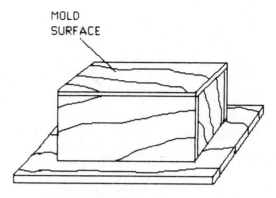

Fig. 11-7. Wood mold for laminating box shape with smooth inside or concave side.

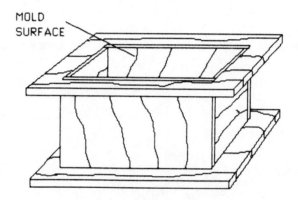

Fig. 11-8. Wood mold for contact molding box form with smooth outside or convex surface.

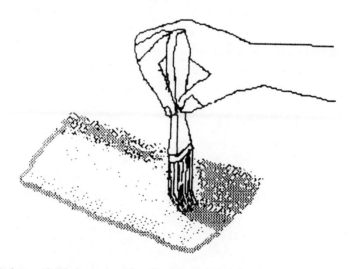

Fig. 11-9. A smooth thin layer of catalyzed polyester resin is brushed on wood molding surface.

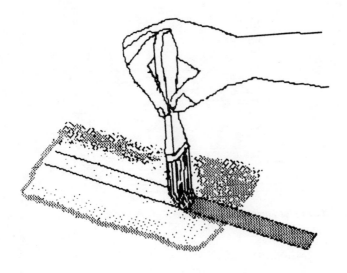

Fig. 11-10. Gel coat is applied to mold surface with long continuous strokes of brush.

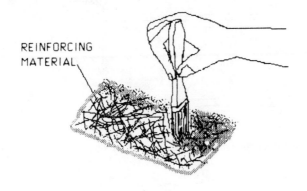

Fig. 11-11. Reinforcing material is saturated with resin.

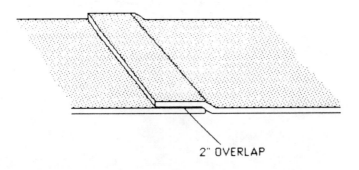

Fig. 11-12. Reinforcing material joined with overlap.

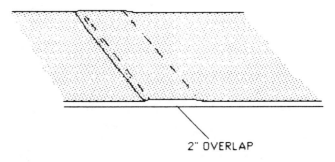

2" OVERLAP

Fig. 11-13. Mat overlap worked down to near even thickness.

FORMING DEEP RECTANGULAR FORMS BY PRESSURE MOLDING

Basic methods for pressure molding shallow and medium-depth rectangular forms were introduced in Chapter 8. We will now expand on these.

Deep Rectangular Double Molds

The bottom half of a double deep rectangular mold is the same as for a single deep rectangular contact mold, as detailed above. For our purposes, we will consider the concave part of the mold as the bottom section and the convex part as the upper section, because this is the position they are usually in for molding so that the resin does not run out of the mold (Fig. 11-14). The upper half of the mold matches the shape of the lower section (they fit together), except that space must be left for the molding. The space varies depending on the particular project, but 1/8 to 1/4 inch is typical.

Because pressure molding gives a smooth surface on both sides, it is important to have the two parts of the mold match each other, minus the desired thickness of the laminate. While the laminate does not necessarily have to be the same thickness throughout, varying the thickness can make molding much more difficult. All of the projects detailed in this chapter for deep rectangular molds can be made with an even thickness of the laminate. Smooth surfaces on both sides allow the mold to be used like a pan or lid, depending on the specific project you are making.

Figure 11-8 shows a wood mold suitable for molding the outside surface of a box form. Figure 11-15 shows the matching section of a wood mold suitable for molding the inside surface of the box form.

Now follow the basic instructions in Chapter 6, Steps 1 through 11. In Step 6, refer to Fig. 11-9.

Pressure Molding Deep Rectangular Forms

To pressure mold a deep rectangular form in the double mold (Fig. 10-16), you will need the items on the materials list, plus a cement building block or other suitable weight for applying pressure to the upper mold sur-

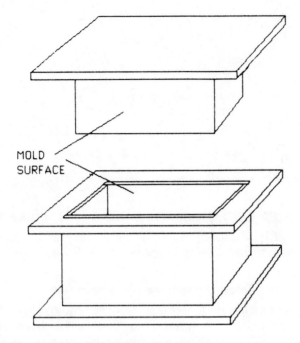

Fig. 11-14. Double mold for pressure molding box form.

face, or C clamps that can be used around the edges to hold the two
mold parts together under pressure.

Now follow the basic instructions, Steps 12 through 32.

In Step 16, refer to Fig. 11-10.

In Step 23, refer to Fig. 11-11.

In Step 27, after turning the upper half of the mold so that the cured
gel coat surface is face down, press it in place on top of the wet layer
of fiberglass reinforcing material. Apply pressure downward and rock
the upper section of the mold back and forth to work out any air. Place
the cement building block or blocks or other suitable weight on top of

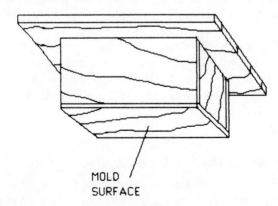

Fig. 11-15. Upper section of double mold made from wood.

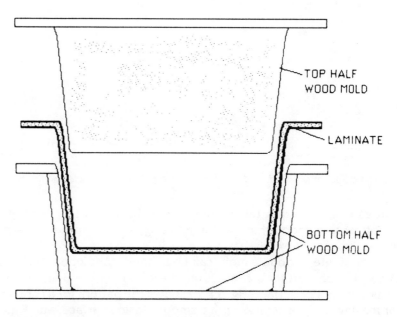

Fig. 11-16. Pressure molding box form in double mold.

the upper half of the mold or use C clamps to hold the mold parts together under pressure. Make sure that the upper half of the mold is level
so that the laminate will have an equal thickness in all areas. Then go
on to Steps 31 and 32.

PROJECTS

Deep Rectangular Planter Box

A deep rectangular planter (Fig. 11-17) can be contact or double molded.
Even though double molding is more difficult, the more attractive planter

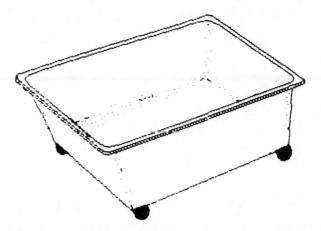

Fig. 11-17. Deep rectangular planter.

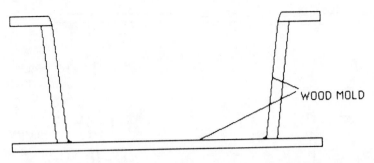

Fig. 11-18. Pattern for wood mold for contact molding deep rectangular planter box.

that can be molded in this manner might be worth the extra effort. It is not recommended that double molding be attempted for large size planter boxes, however.

The single or double mold can be shaped from wood. Figure 11-18 shows the pattern for a contact mold for making the planter box with a smooth outside surface; Fig. 11-19 shows the pattern for a contact mold for making the planter box with a smooth inside surface; and Fig. 11-20 shows the pattern for a two-part pressure mold for making the box smooth both inside and outside.

Construct and prepare a suitable mold and contact or pressure mold the box using the methods detailed previously.

After the planter box laminate has cured, remove it from the mold. Saw off excess fiberglass from edges of laminate and file and sand edges smooth, rounding them slightly.(These instructions apply to the rest of the projects in this chapter.)

Finish the planter by attaching suitable legs or pods.

Deep Rectangular Wastebasket

A deep rectangular wastebasket is shown in Fig. 11-21.

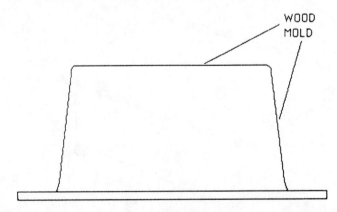

Fig. 11-19. Pattern for wood mold for contact molding deep rectangular planter box with smooth interior surface.

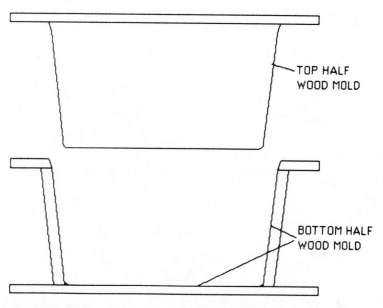

Fig. 11-20. Pattern for double mold for deep rectangular planter box.

Shape the single or double mold from wood, using the methods detailed previously. Figure 11-22 shows the pattern for a contact mold for making the wastebasket with a smooth outside surface; Fig. 11-23 shows the pattern for a contact mold for making the wastebasket with a smooth inside surface (giving a rough outside surface for decorative effect); and Fig. 11-24 shows the pattern for a two-part pressure mold for making the wastebasket smooth both inside and outside.

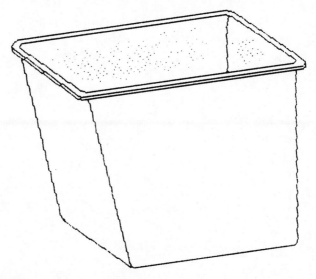

Fig. 11-21. Deep rectangular wastebasket.

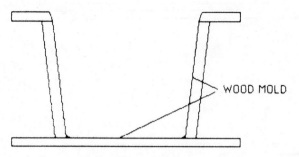

Fig. 11-22. Pattern for wood mold for contact molding deep rectangular wastebasket with smooth outside surface.

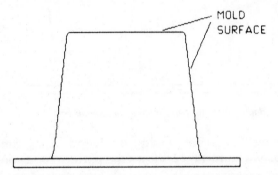

Fig. 11-23. Pattern for wood mold for contact molding deep rectangular wastebasket with smooth interior surface.

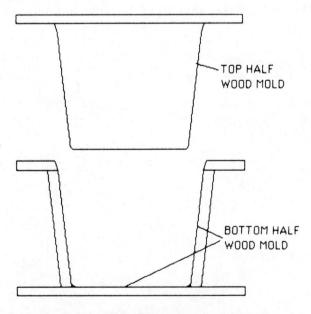

Fig. 11-24. Pattern for double mold for deep rectangular wastebasket.

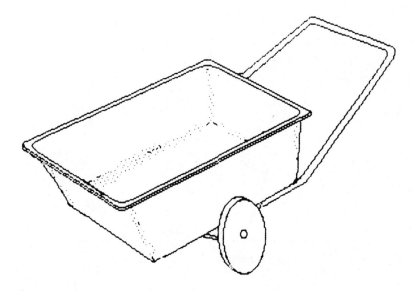

Fig. 11-25. Garden cart.

Garden Cart

A molded fiberglass garden cart is shown in Fig. 11-25.

Shape the single or double mold from wood, using the methods detailed previously in this chapter. Refer to Figs. 11-18, 11-19, and 11-20 for illustrations of these molds. Although the finished products are different, the molds are very similar.

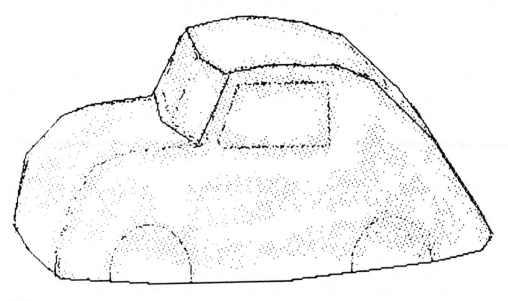

Fig. 11-26. Toy car body.

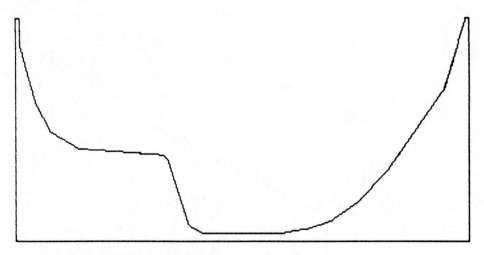

Fig. 11-27. Contact mold for toy car body.

Finish the garden cart by adding suitable wheel and axle assembly and handles.

Toy Car Body

A toy car body (Fig. 11-26) can be molded to desired size, from a small model to a toy car that children can ride in. In most cases, the toy car

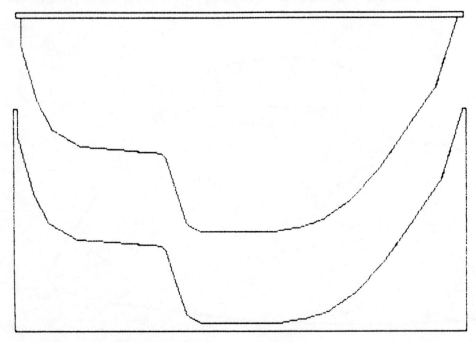

Fig. 11-28. Double mold for toy car body.

Fig. 11-29. Smooth gel coat side of contact molded air scoop.

body will be contact molded, with the outside surface of the car body the smooth side.

Shape the single or double mold from wood. Figure 11-27 shows the pattern for a contact mold for making the car body with a smooth outside surface and Fig. 11-28 shows the pattern for a two-part pressure mold for making the molding smooth both inside and outside.

Construct and prepare a suitable mold, and contact or pressure mold the toy car body. Remove the laminate from the mold after it has cured. Saw off excess fiberglass from laminate, saw out windows and other openings as required, and file and sand edges smooth, rounding them slightly.

Other Projects Using Deep Rectangular Moldings

Using the same methods detailed above, a variety of other projects are possible using the same basic molding form, including an air scoop (Figs. 11-29 and 11-30), a radio case (Fig. 11-31), and a suitcase, which uses two separate moldings (Fig. 11-32).

Fig. 11-30. Backside (side away from mold) of contact molded air scoop.

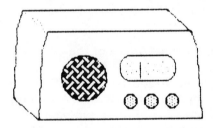

Fig. 11-31. Radio case.

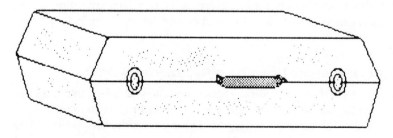

Fig. 11-32. Suitcase.

Chapter 12

Miscellaneous Molding Techniques and Projects

A variety of interesting projects are possible using combinations of techniques detailed previously in this book and other miscellaneous techniques.

All of the projects detailed previously in this book have used constructed or existing molds. There are many situations, however, where it is desirable to duplicate an existing object or where it is easier to make a mock-up of something to duplicate than to make the mold in reverse image form. Essentially, you make the form of the desired object. Then you duplicate it, using the actual item or mock-up as a form or mold to make a mold.

Making duplicates of existing items in fiberglass are interesting and challenging projects. One popular use of this technique is to make automobile fenders and other body parts, using original parts for making the molds for the duplicates. A number of businesses have been established that make duplicate body parts and even complete bodies for antique cars.

DUPLICATING AN EXISTING OBJECT

In previous chapters, when you used bowls, pans, and other existing items as molds, you molded a reverse image of the object rather than making a duplicate of the mold. This is much easier than duplicating the mold. However, there are situations where only a duplicate will work.

For example, if you have a cracked plastic typewriter case lid, such as shown in Fig. 12-1, using either the outside or inside of the lid as a mold will not result in a duplicate. The molding you take off the top side of the lid will be larger than the original lid. The molding you take off the inside of the lid will result in a lid that is smaller than the original. Neither molding will fit the original typewriter case.

While the molds can be made from a variety of materials such as plaster or clay, a fiberglass laminate generally gives better results.

Making a Contact Mold

To make a fiberglass contact mold of an existing form, you will need an object suitable for duplicating, as detailed above, and items 2 through 12 on the materials list in Chapter 6.

Place the object to be duplicated on the protective paper with the surface to be copied upward. If the surface to be copied is concave, you will do the layup inside a pan form. If the surface to be copied is convex, you will do the layup over a cap-like form. Make certain that the item to be duplicated is suitable for molding. There should be no overhangs that will make it difficult or impossible to remove the mold from the item being duplicated. For our purposes here, we will assume that you are making a duplicate of the typewriter case lid shown in Fig. 12-1. Because contact molding gives only one smooth side to the molding, you will want to take your mold from the upper outer surface of the lid. In this way when you later use the mold for contact molding a new lid, you will have the smooth gel coat side on the outside of the case. Later in this chapter, we will cover double molding techniques, which will duplicate both sides of the object.

Once you are satisfied that the object is suitable for duplicating, apply a coat of the paste-type mold release, using a clean cloth to spread a thin layer of the release over the entire mold surface. This will keep the molding from sticking so that it can be removed after it has cured. Figure 12-2 shows mold release being applied to the typewriter case lid.

Apply the tooling gel coat on the typewriter lid over the mold release. A color of gel coat resin is often selected for the mold that will contrast sharply with the gel coat color that will be used later for making moldings with the mold.

Now follow the base instructions in Chapter 6, Steps 15 through 31.

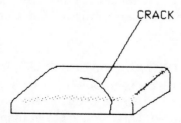

CRACK

Fig. 12-1. Cracked typewriter case lid.

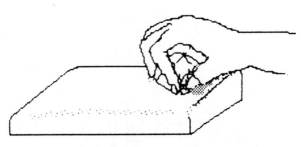

Fig. 12-2. Mold release is applied.

In Step 16, refer to Fig. 12-3.

In Step 17, cuts with lap joints are usually required to form the dry mat to the approximate shape of the deep rectangular form and compound curves.

In Step 23, refer to Fig. 12-4.

In Step 24, refer to Figs. 12-5 and 12-6.

Some fiberglass molds will require trimming. First mark pattern and saw off excess fiberglass, as required. Sawing methods are detailed in Chapter 5. In some cases a stand or base is attached to the fiberglass mold. Some molds require additional reinforcement on the back side of the laminate (this is not necessary for the typewriter case lid or other similar small molds). One method of doing this is to bond plywood frames to the laminate with fiberglass bonding strips (Fig. 12-7).

Polish and buff the gel coat surfaces. The mold is then ready for contact molding a duplicate of the item being copied.

Making a Double Mold

Again, keep in mind that double molding is usually only practical for duplicating relatively small objects. As detailed above, the contact mold forms half of the double mold. To make a fiberglass mold of the oppo-

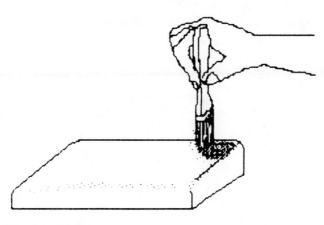

Fig. 12-3. Gel coat is applied.

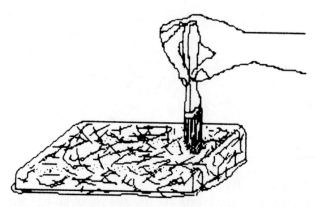

Fig. 12-4. Reinforcing material is saturated with resin.

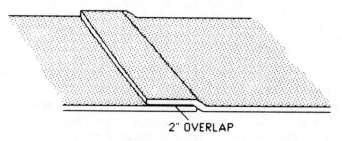

2" OVERLAP

Fig. 12-5. Reinforcing material joined with overlap.

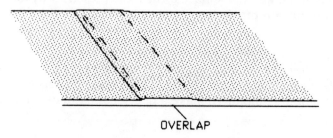

OVERLAP

Fig. 12-6. Mat overlap worked down to near even thickness.

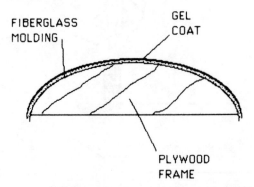

FIBERGLASS
MOLDING

GEL
COAT

PLYWOOD
FRAME

Fig. 12-7. Plywood frame fiberglass bonded to back side of laminate.

190

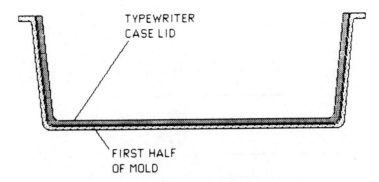

TYPEWRITER
CASE LID

FIRST HALF
OF MOLD

Fig. 12-8. Lid is placed like a pan with first half of mold in place.

site side of an existing object, you will need the object suitable for duplicating and the first half of the double mold, as well as items 2 through 14 on the materials list. Use gel coat tooling resin for item 4.

Place the object to be duplicated and the first half of the mold on the protective paper with the surface to be copied as the second half of the mold upward. If the surface to be copied is concave, you will do the layup inside a pan form. If the surface to be copied is convex, you will do the layup over a cap-like form. For the typewriter case example, the upper surface of the lid was already copied. The lid is now placed like a pan with the first half of the mold in place (Fig. 12-8). The second half of the mold is then laid up inside the lid. Again, make sure there are no overhangs that will make it difficult to remove the mold from the item being duplicated.

Apply a coat of the paste-type mold release to the new molding surface, using a clean cloth to spread a thin layer of the release over the entire mold surface. Figure 12-9 shows mold release being applied to the inside of the typewriter case lid.

Apply the tooling gel coat to the inside of the typewriter lid over the mold release. Open the container of gel coat polyester resin and carefully stir it.

Now, follow the basic instructions, Steps 15 through 31.

In Step 16, refer to Fig. 12-10.

In Step 22, refer to Fig. 12-11.

In Step 24, refer to Figs. 12-5 and 12-6.

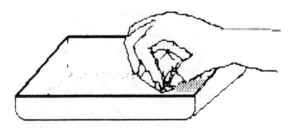

Fig. 12-9. Mold release is applied.

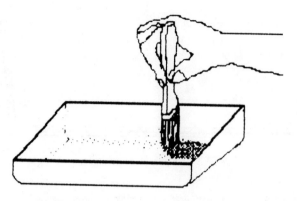

Fig. 12-10. Gel coat is applied.

After completing Step 31, keep in mind that some molds require additional reinforcement on the back side of the laminate (this would not be necessary for the typewriter case lid mold parts or other similar small molds).

Polish and buff the gel coat surfaces. The mold is then ready for pressure molding a duplicate of the item being copied. Double molding methods are the same as detailed in previous chapters.

MAKING MOCK-UPS

In many cases, no existing item is available for duplicating. In this situation, it is often possible to make a mock-up that is suitable for duplication techniques. Essentially, you then use the mock-up as a form for making the mold. The question might well be asked, why not just make the mold itself directly? This method was used for most of the projects detailed previously in this book, and for simple shapes and forms, it is usually the easiest and best method to use. However, as the mold shapes become more complicated, it becomes much more difficult to work with a reverse image. A mock-up, which will look just like the desired finished

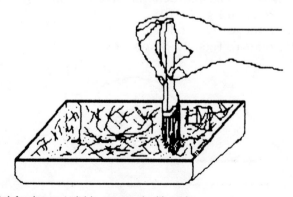

Fig. 12-11. Reinforcing material is saturated with resin.

object, makes sense, even though it is an extra step to obtaining the mold itself.

Mock-ups can be made from a variety of materials. One method is to use plaster, which is reinforced with burlap material in the same way resin and fiberglass reinforcing material is used. Before laminating fiberglass over the plaster surface, it should first be sealed with a coat of catalyzed resin or other suitable sealer. The surface is then sanded and polished so it is suitable for making a fiberglass mold.

Mock-ups can also be shaped from a single piece of wood or, more typically, from two or more pieces of wood glued together. Ordinary woodworking techniques are used for shaping deep rectangular molds from wood. Figure 12-12 shows a wood mock-up for an air scoop.

Now follow the basic instructions, Steps 2 through 10.

Any defects in the molding surface will be copied onto the mold made from it, which in turn will be copied on the moldings made from the mold. In some cases, it is possible to make corrections and repairs to the surface of the mold, but this is usually easier done on the mock-up so that no changes will be required on the mold.

After a suitable mock-up has been made and prepared, the mold can then be fiberglass laminated using the mock-up as a "mold."

LARGE MOLDINGS

Fiberglass laminating and molding is generally best learned by beginning with small moldings and gradually working up to larger ones. While large moldings are not necessarily any more difficult, the materials and time investments are larger. It is much better to mess up a small project involving a minimum amount of materials than a large one.

A variety of large molding projects are possible using the techniques detailed in this book, such as a shower stall (Fig. 12-13), a bathtub (Fig. 12-14), a hot tub (Fig. 12-15), or a garden pond (Fig. 12-16).

Large projects are usually contact molded to give a smooth finish on one side only, or simply laid up over a form without any molded surface. Such is the case for a garden pond where a smooth surface is not required.

Large contact molds can be constructed from wood, metal, fiberglass, plaster, and a variety of other materials the same way smaller projects are, except that they are made larger and require more materials.

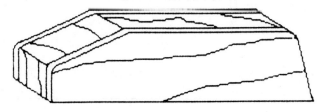

Fig. 12-12. Wood mock-up for air scoop.

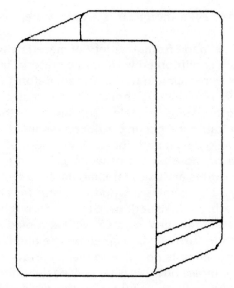

Fig. 12-13. Shower stall.

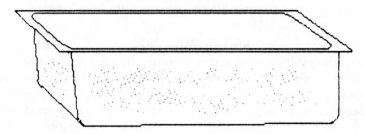

Fig. 12-14. Bathtub.

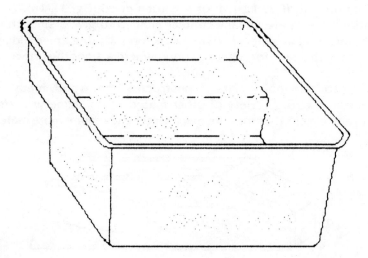

Fig. 12-15. Hot tub.

194

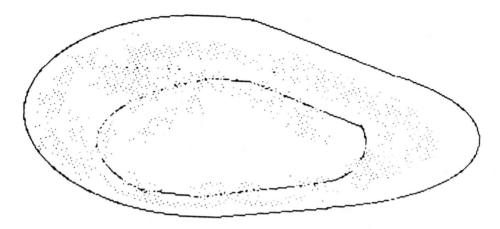

Fig. 12-16. Garden pond.

If a mold is to be used for one molding only, it doesn't need to be as strong as a re-usable mold.

Laminating a Large Contact Molding

To laminate a large contact molding, you will need the items on the materials list.

The mold should be positioned so that as much of the laminating as possible can be done on a level or near-level plane. If the mold is concave, such as for the car body shown in Fig. 12-17, you will do the lay-up inside a pan form. If the mold is convex, such as for a bathtub (Fig. 12-18), you will do the lay-up over a cap-like form. Make certain that the mold is suitable. There should be no overhangs that will make it difficult or impossible to remove the molding from the mold. An exception to this is when a temporary mold is used for making one molding only, in which case the mold can be destroyed to get it out of the molding.

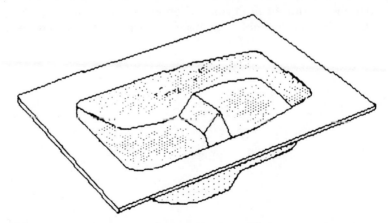

Fig. 12-17. Contact mold for car body in position for molding.

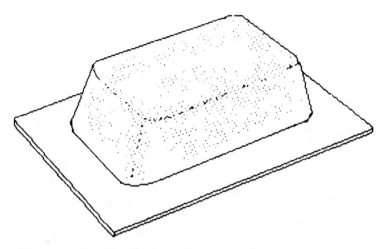

Fig. 12-18. Contact mold for bathtub in position for molding.

Apply a coat of the paste-type mold release, using a clean cloth to spread a thin layer of the release over the entire mold surface (Fig. 12-19). The purpose of this is to keep the molding from sticking to the mold so that it can be removed after it has cured.

Now follow the basic instructions, Steps 14 through 31.

In Step 16, refer to Fig. 12-20.

In Step 20, you will probably need about 15 (rather than 7 1/2 minutes of working time to apply the resin to a single layer of reinforcing material or one strip of material for a very large mold; more time may be required for multiple layers.

In Step 23, refer to Fig. 12-21.

In Step 24, a squeegee or laminating roller can be used to remove air bubbles. For joining separate pieces of reinforcing material, the basic technique is to overlap the pieces 2 to 6 inches (Fig. 12-5). If mat is used, the laminate can be worked down to a nearly even thickness with a dabbing action of the brush when applying resin to the overlap (Fig. 12-6). For most large moldings, however, this is not really necessary.

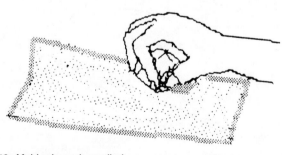

Fig. 12-19. Mold release is applied.

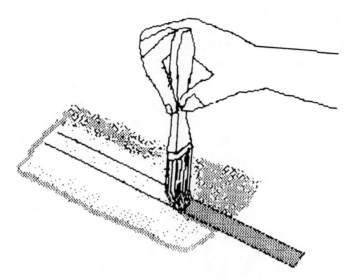

Fig. 12-20. Gel coat is applied to mold surface with long continuous strokes of brush.

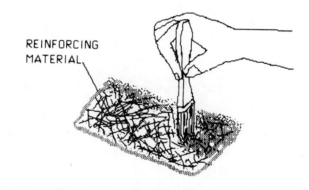

REINFORCING
MATERIAL

Fig. 12-21. Reinforcing material is saturated with resin.

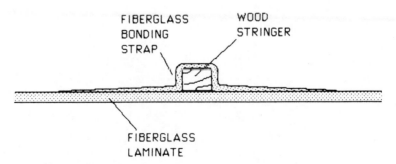

FIBERGLASS
BONDING
STRAP

WOOD
STRINGER

FIBERGLASS
LAMINATE

Fig. 12-22. Wood stringer used to reinforce fiberglass laminate.

197

Some moldings require additional reinforcement on the back side of the laminate. One method of doing this is to bond stringers to the laminate with fiberglass bonding strips (Fig. 12-22).

Polish and buff the gel coat surfaces.

Appendix

Appendix

Suppliers

Mail-Order Fiberglassing Materials and Supplies

Clark Craft
16-R1 Aqualane
Tonawanda, NY 14150

Polyester and epoxy resins; fiberglass cloth, mat, and woven roving; plastic foams; etc.

Defender Industries, Inc.
255 Main St.
New Rochelle, NY 10801

Offers complete line of fiberglassing materials and supplies at discount prices.

Glen-L
9152 Rosecrans
Bellflower, CA 90706

Complete line of fiberglassing materials and supplies.

Other Fiberglassing Material and Supply Sources

Fibre Glass Evercoat
  Company
6600 Cornell Rd.
Cincinnati, OH 45242

Resin, fiberglass reinforcing materials, and filler materials.

Lan-O-Sheen
1 W. Water St.
St. Paul, MN 55107

Resin and fiberglass reinforcing materials.

Oatey Company 4700 W. 160th St. Cleveland, OH 44135	*Fiberglassing materials.*
Pettit Paint Company, Inc. 30 Pine St. Rockaway, NJ 07866	*Polyurethane paint, resins, and fiberglass reinforcing materials. Fiberglassing materials.*
Plastic Sales and Manu- facturing Company, Inc. 3030 McGee Trafficway Kansas City, MO 64108	*Polyester and epoxy resins and fiberglass reinforcing materials.*
Ram Chemicals 210 E. Alondra Rd. Gardena, CA 90248	*Gel coat resins and release agents*
Rule Industries, Inc. Cape Ann Industrial Park Gloucester, MA 01930	*Resins and fiberglass reinforcing materials.*

Glossary

Glossary

accelerator—A highly active oxidizing material such as cobalt, that is added to polyester resin to produce internal heat, so the resin will cure at room temperature.

acetone—A cleaning solvent for removing uncured resin from brushes and tools.

air-inhibited resin—A resin in which the presence of air will inhibit the cure of the surface. The surface usually becomes hard but is tacky.

ambient temperature—Surrounding temperature or "room" temperature.

barrier cream—A skin cream used to protect the skin from possible contact with resins.

binder—An adhesive that in soluble is resin and is used to loosely bind glass fibers together to form fiberglass mat.

catalyst—Component added to polyester resin to initiate the curing, usually by oxidizing an accelerator.

cavity—A female mold or the laminating space between matched molds.

chopped strands—Glass fiber strands chopped up into short lengths.

close weave—Reinforcing fabric with the woven strands almost touching.

color pigments—Pigments that are added to resin to change its color.

core—Material used between two fiberglass skins to space them apart and give greater stiffness.

crazing—Tiny cracks in the surface of a fiberglass molding.

cure — The process of resin changing from a liquid to a solid state.

cure time — The time between adding the catalyst or hardener to a resin and the resin reaching a cured state.

epoxy resin — A resin that is stronger and has better physical properties than polyester resin, but is more difficult to use and considerably more expensive.

exothermic heat — Developed within the resin.

feathered edge — Tapered edge of fiberglass laminate.

fiberglass — Fine fibers of glass; reinforcing materials made from glass fibers; laminates of glass fiber reinforcing material and cured resin.

filler — Substance added to resin to form a putty; a resin filler or putty.

finish — Applied to glass fibers to allow resin to flow around and adhere to the fibers.

foam — A rigid plastic material that is very light in weight.

foam core — Foam used as a core material between two skins of fiberglass.

gel — A semi-solid or jellylike state of resin when partially cured.

gel coat — Surface coat of resin that does not contain glass fibers and is usually colored.

glass fibers — A fine fiber of glass.

hardener — Component added to epoxy resin to initiate the curing.

lamination — Layers of glass reinforcing materials and resin that form a fiberglass panel.

lay-up — Process of applying resin to reinforcing materials placed in a mold.

mold — Form used for fiberglass lay-up to give desired shape and surface.

mold release — Substance used to prevent molding from sticking in the mold.

molding — Cured fiberglass object that has been formed in a mold.

non-air-inhibited resin — A resin that gives a surface cure in the presence of air by excluding air from the surface of the resin.

open weave — Reinforcing fabric with considerable space between woven strands.

plain weave — Common over-under weave used for making fabrics.

plastics — Synthetic materials; sometimes used to mean "fiberglass."

polyester resin — Resin commonly combined with reinforcing materials to form fiberglass. Because of lower cost, it is usually used instead of more expensive epoxy resin.

pot life—The length of time that a resin remains usable in a container after catalyst or hardening agent has been added.

putty—A resin filler material.

release agent—A coating applied to mold to prevent molding from sticking to the mold.

resin—A liquid plastic substance that cures to a hard substance when a catalyst or hardener is added; combined with reinforcing materials to form fiberglass.

roving—Continuous strands of glass fibers used to form untwisted yarn, which can be woven into woven roving reinforcing material.

sandwich construction—A core material with fiberglass skins.

shelf life—The length of time uncatalyzed resin will remain usable when stored in a sealed container; also applies to paints and other substances.

styrene—Liquid plastic used to thin polyester resin.

surfacing agent—Oil or wax material that goes to the surface of polyester resin during cure to inhibit air.

tack-free—A surface that is not sticky.

tacky—Sticky.

thixotropic—A liquid that has a high viscosity so that it will not flow easily.

thixotropic paste or powder—Added to resin to increase viscosity.

undercut—Reverse draft in a mold.

unidirectional—Strength is mainly in one direction; often applied to a reinforcing material that is woven to give greater strength in one direction than another.

vacuum bag molding—A method of molding that uses a flexible bag and a vacuum.

viscosity—Degree to which a liquid resists flow.

warp—Fibers woven across a fabric.

woven roving—Reinforcing fabric woven from strands of rovings, which are untwisted groups of glass fibers.

yarn—Twisted strands of glass fibers that are woven to form cloth.

Index

Index

211